Talent

Tools

Time

Treasure

Talent

Tools

Time

Treasure

A Prosperity Decision Guide

The TCRE 4Ts - Leverage the Talent, Tools, Time & Treasure needed for Decisioning, Success & Prosperity.

TalentCRE Inc., Publisher

ISBN 978-0-578-99009-5

CONTENTS

"The hardest part in life is making a decision, the easy part is following a proven success plan."

_____

"Integrity, always do the right thing and always do what you say you're going to do."

Introduction

We first want to say thank you to you, for choosing to invest your most precious commodity time and for being an inquisitive person who is open to learning and to applying our culmination of proven unique success strategies. We also want to thank the countless Family, Friends, Teachers, Mentors, Authors, Industry Professionals and Clients that have given us the insights and life experience necessary to develop personally and professionally.

Our goal is to provide you with a Personal and Professional success book/ field guide that you can model and personalize to help you live an extraordinary life as your true self, full of self-love.

Why is this so important to us? For me Wick, it starts with my childhood growing up in an entrepreneurial family, my first memories at five years old are standing at the parts counter of my father's mechanic shop C&W Imports. While he was in the garage back-bay wrenching on foreign sports cars I would be up front answering the phone and helping customers when they came in, granted my contribution was small but was it really? Being, the first face everyone saw when they came through the doors of the shop was a very important job and let me tell you I got some interesting reactions from laughs, turn arounds, dismissive expressions and general what is wrong with this picture looks. But surprisingly I was able to win them over with a friendly smile and asking how can I help you? This would prove to be the beginning of what I would eventually learn was to become my vocation in life – To Help People Personally and Professionally.

Now it took me quite a long time and quite a few first perceived failures to come to this realization. I know everyone will appreciate the quick snapshot version which led me too here and now. My early years were spent working in my family businesses, my father's business which was Import Cars Service, Motorcycle Sales & Service and Boat Sales & Service and my uncle's Investment Banking Firm in Boston. At sixteen I started to build on my interest in construction and apprenticed as a finish carpenter and flooring mechanic. Continuing to work in the trades while attending college I decided to stop my formal education at age twenty and start my first Company, a floor contracting business in Massachusetts which I would eventually successfully relocate to Florida where I partnered with a National Insurance and Fire and Water Restoration Franchise. This allowed me to expand my reach into all facets of construction including general contracting, design build, residential renovations, commercial tenant improvement, spec building and real estate development through multiple successful ventures, then cue the great recession of 2007.

I had a decision to make, wind down my speculative and future development projects and go backwards to focus on recession proof small renovation projects or wind down everything and start a new path consulting for Architectural and Construction firms. I choose the ladder which focused on helping firms navigate the extremely low demand recession environment by refining their operations so they would come out of the recession stronger with a long-term profitable business model. This proved to be very challenging but extremely enlightening on how many businesses just work blindly with no clear strategy, no real visibility into actual numbers or have the tools necessary combined with actionable plans to ensure business success. It also provided an introduction, to some of the largest Global Commercial Real Estate Firms and key decision makers that those businesses serviced. Next pivotal step identified, vocation becoming clearer.

My target company and role were set, and through my network I was able to secure a meeting with the Division President of the World's largest Commercial Real Estate Firm. It was a very humbling meeting to say the least, I thought I was poised to slide right into a Senior Level role where I would be running a multi-service client engagement for one of their high-profile global clients. Instead, I was given an invaluable gift that day, he gave me absolute honesty on how I would not be successful and took the time to educate me on why I was not ready. Explaining to me that even though I had proven myself to be a great business leader, in their unique business I would not even know or understand the requirements of their corporate clients, all the vocabulary, the terms, acronyms, rules of engagement, compliance, sector specific solutions, etc... With that said do I think you can learn it and learn it quickly – Yes. See he had a similar construction background as me and knew exactly the best action plan to implement that would put me into the best position to succeed. Then as a parting gift he informed me of a perceived low-level role that was coming available and connected me with the service line Senior Leader who was running it where I could leverage my construction experience to put me on the fast-track to becoming a Commercial Real Estate Services (CRE) Account Leader.

I was fortunate to go onto win that first role in CRE Services as Project Management team lead for a Global Bank that had acquired a US Northeast Region bank network that was required to complete a compliance driven fast-track schedule rebrand. The participation and success of delivering that program enable me to learn the unique nuances of the CRE Services world as well as provided me the access, education and opportunity path for the next decade at the two largest Global CRE firms, which included varied business sector client engagements on high risk, high profile programs including multi-service-line advisory and delivery of Global Corporate Solutions; Transaction Management, Workplace Strategy, Occupancy Planning, Construction Project Management and Facilities Management.

It also became a proving ground for my unique solutions and turned my mindset from service provider to strategic partner, where the focus would be understanding all facets of the client business and implementing strategies that helped them achieve all of their company objectives, talent (employee) satisfaction, company culture, branding, client satisfaction, increased profitability, change management (communication) and future-cast actionable strategies based on past performance with success data driven refinements.

But the most impactful aspect of my CRE journey and what truly solidified my vocation of helping people personally and professionally was meeting my now business partner and co-author Pablo Sierra on one of my last client engagements, which ultimately led to the founding of TalentCRE, Inc in 2020 (the most dynamic and challenging year of modern times since 1968), where all of our collective experience and business transcending purpose exists: That Everyone be Valued and Treated as a Unique Asset.

I am compelled to detour from our outline, as I was completing my writing session at 3:00am est. January 7th, 2021 the US congress was simultaneously certifying the 2020 US election of President elect Joe Biden and Vice President elect Kamala Harris the first female African American, Indian American and first person of Asian American decent to be elected. This monumental event was attempted to be overshadowed and blocked by one of the lowest historical events in our 245year Democracy, the violent fatal riots and occupation of the US Capital Building by the defeated candidate insurrectionists at 3:00pm est. on January 6th, 2021. I believe our purpose has never been more relevant in my lifetime and I have never been more certain, energized and convinced of the importance of succeeding in my vocation, writing this book and doing everything in my power to help everyone I can personally and professionally.

My hope is that you live the extraordinary life you were intended and that the ideas, life lessons and proven actionable strategies in the chapters to follow will inspire, energize and give you the foundation to realize your greatest dreams.

For me Pablo, a few years ago while working at my bookstore, a customer came in, stopped in the front entrance for a few moments and began to wander around, getting lost in the aisles of books. Of course, I knew where he was without having to follow and "accidentally" bumped into him after about 3 minutes of letting him explore. "Hey, how are you doing? Can I help you with anything?" "No," he said, "Just looking. Great spot you got here. Smells like wood." I did not press but saw him looking in the business section and obviously asked, "Looking for something special in business?" That opened the flood gates and as it was a random Tuesday afternoon with no customers, there was time to talk. During the conversation, he revealed that his personal and professional life just was not going his way – he felt "off track" and did not know how to get back there, or if he was ever on the right track in the first place. He had dreams and thoughts about how his life should be and frankly, it was not there. In fact, during the conversation, he laughed and said, "You know, actually I am grateful for a lot of things, but I can't help but feel that I'm capable of more. That I should be more than what my current situation shows."

We continued to talk and he admitted that thoughts of the past, present and future inundated his mind, making it difficult to make sense of it all and develop an understanding of what has happened, the impacts of those events to his future and the steps to address the situation.

We shared our experience's and I recommended a few books in the personal development section, business section and literature area that I thought could address what was on his mind, books that helped me. But in the end, all he was looking for was a simple framework and guidelines to take home, assess his life, develop plans and implement his dreams.

This book provides that framework and guidelines. It is a way forward, either out of the current muck or a refinement of an already great situation. It will provide a way to take a step back, look at things both subjectively and objectively, create a plan using a solid framework and then develop real action items to implement that plan. The result will be a feeling of more control and a greater awareness of self and the environment to make better assessments, develop plans and have the confidence to implement those plans.

I have experienced the same thoughts of needing control, needing a plan, needing guidance – because, like all of us, I have dreams too. Dreams for myself, my family, the world, and I want to see those dreams become a reality. And maybe more importantly, I want to be prepared for the reality of those dreams, not surprised and unprepared to handle the responsibilities of success.

I wake to a blessed life - having great parents, sisters and family, an awesome wife and child, good health (a great head of hair when I was younger), fantastic personal experiences traveling the world, proudly served in the Navy, a love of reading and an insatiable desire to experience life and God, in all His forms. I have also been in substantial debt, suffered business failures, broken relationships and experience an ever-questioning belief and faith in God.

That questioning faith and desire to experience the life God wants me to have can be a double-edged sword. That desire causes me to constantly seek out a better way to lead my life and make those experiences reality. My father was a Special Forces Green Beret, but I do not come from a military family, yet went to the Naval Academy wanting to be physically, mentally, and morally challenged to become "something." I have started a business, a bookstore, with limited business experience to do "something." I have moved from profession to profession, in search of a position where I could exercise my God-given talents and have "something." Each time thwarted by my wanderlust and difficulty in being happy in the moment.

I wanted more but never quite knew what that more was or how to get it. That journey led to a passion for personal and professional development – the processes and tools to find that "something," to get that "more." My innate organizational and engineering self-led me to project management – the technical methodologies of seeing a problem, analyzing it, and then utilizing a framework to break that problem down into components. This book is that framework and more. A framework to answer the question, "What's going on?" then go further and develop real, actionable activities based on that answer.

There are many Authors with books addressing the challenges of seeking the ever better self. Books with their own processes and guidelines in one way or another. As a former bookseller , I cannot help but tell you to read those as well. From Proverbs in the Bible, and other religious texts of wisdom, to Ben Franklin's Autobiography and everything published from that point forward. Read those books and choose the information that speaks to you. The same things might be said but when said differently, at different times of your life, you will get a different message and perspective. Read them, think about them and act on them. Of course, add us to that list and go forward with tools from as many experts as you can find.

As Thoreau said, "Go confidently in the direction of your dreams. Live the life you've imagined." Let the frameworks and guidelines in this book fuel your continuous process of improvement and help you live that life you have imagined.

1

TCRE 4Ts Methodology

After spending hours upon hours of delivering programs/ projects with varied teams of people from all different backgrounds, experience levels and own personal agendas it became very clear to us that there was one key factor that always determined the outcome. It was **Talent,** the key to any successful endeavor or demise came down to the person and who they really are regarding rapport, respect, rectitude (integrity/ honesty/ moral character), ethics and their sense of responsibility, commitment and level of investment they put into everything they do. Now you probably noticed that we left out Talent's education, experience and expertise in their chosen field in this assessment checklist. The reason for this is that if the people you are counting on do not possess all these first characteristics at the highest level, then it will make no difference how smart or experienced, they are, your collective endeavors will suffer and never be as successful or even worse could lead to a disastrous outcome.

Here are two examples that illustrate both:

o   **Disaster – Bernie Madoff**

In 2009, Bernie Madoff an American Financier who executed the largest Ponzi scheme in history pleaded guilty to 11 federal felonies, including securities fraud, wire fraud, mail fraud, money laundering, making false statements, perjury, theft from an employee benefit plan, and making false filings with the SEC. At age 71, he was sentenced to no less than 150 years.

Bernie Madoff understood the financial world, wanted to be a part of it and through his education, network and experience, had the ability to succeed. But there is no doubt that all those attributes were not founded in basic values of integrity and moral

1

character and without those guiding principles to influence thoughts and actions – investors (trusting people) lost their life savings - billions of dollars – and maybe more tragically, peace of mind about the goodness of people.

o   **Success – Maya Angelou**

In a Harlem brownstone, with the conversation among writers, artists and family filling the noise, Maya Angelou would cook down home country recipes learned from her grandmother while the beat of calypso music she used to sing played in the background. And whether it is Thanksgiving Dinner, a Christmas Tree decorating party, New Year's Eve or the celebration of a loved one's accomplishment, the warmth and love Maya displayed in the festivities was fueled by her love and deep respect for the people – and their personal histories of life – who filled her home.

As an African American woman raised in the deep south, the access, education and opportunity needed for what is considered success in society was limited. She lived with various family members throughout her childhood – her father leaving her with her grandmother in Arkansas to back with her father and back again. As a child, she developed an extraordinary memory, a love for books and literature, and an ability to listen and observe the world around her. She also felt the sting of upheaval and experienced tragedies early – including her sexual assault at 8 years old.

Facing racism, sexism, sexual assault and family upheaval, Maya would become one of the most respected, beloved writers and artists of the 20th Century.
She achieved this success due to her values - humility founded by her faith in God, a love of life, family and friends, and a commitment to the truth – the truth about the world and the truth about yourself.

Born April 4, 1928, Maya, raised by her Grandmother, had a multitude of jobs – from being the first female cable car conductor in San Francisco, a dancer, a writer, playwright, and Civil Rights Activist – the list of her work and achievements fills its own book. And Maya, having never earned a bachelor's degree, would rise to the top of the literary world through her commitment to her values and an understanding of the world that requires persistence, optimism and forgiveness.

"All my work, my life, everything I do is about survival, not just bare, awful, plodding survival, but survival with grace and faith. While one may encounter many defeats, one must not be defeated."
- Maya Angelou

We have defined the **first (T) Talent** now let us delve into the other three T's and how they came about and when combined in the SWOT(T) (strengths, weaknesses, opportunities, threats and trends) framework provide one of the most powerful assessment, decision making tools that can be applied across a multitude of business functions, projects and even personal situations.

The TCRE 4Ts Methodology all came together after years of finding ourselves in negative situations with new client engagements or projects that had gone bad or were assigned to us to fix. As such we needed a way to assess the current reality as quick as possible to be able to determine the pros and cons in key influence areas and to form an immediate action plan that had sequential logic and facts to support our go forward strategy. We also needed a way to determine if we were going to be successful in achieving the end goal. What revealed itself every single time was when all 4Ts were strong/ favorable it did not matter the undertaking or situation we found ourselves in, the end goal was always achievable - formation of the TCRE 4Ts.

Second (T) Tools, for most people tools are found in a toolbox in the garage or back in a closet somewhere or thrown in a junk drawer if we have any hand tools at all. These are not the tools we are talking about, although if relevant hand and power tools may make the assessment list especially if they are an integral part to the underlying business or project. For the most part when we use the term tool's we are referring to equipment, standardized processes, content documents, technology platforms, trade specific methods of procedures, workflows and anything and everything required to deliver product and achieve the desired results.

Example of Tools on an Assessment List:

Professional Tools
Technology - Computers/ Smartphones Software/ Security
Manufacturing/ Logistics Platform
Diagnostic/ Testing Equipment
Personal Protection Equipment (PPE)
Specialty Machinery/ Vehicles
Operations Manuals/ Procedures
Marketing/ Advertising Content
Leads Source Lists/ Sales Scripts
Playbooks/ Project Mgmt. Processes
Workplace Standards/ Guidelines

Third (T) Time, we know time is our most valuable commodity and as it pertains to our personal and professional lives there is no clearer defined parameter on what we can accomplish. Personally, we have a finite amount of time on this planet to experience all of life's wonderful gifts (failures and successes), time to grow into our true selves, time spending with family and friends, time discovering things we love to do and time achieving all our

Foundational Goals (FG's) – more to come on this key component to an extraordinary life.

Professionally everything is about time, speed to market, speed to delivery, speed to respond, speed to new ideas and just straight faster, faster, faster with seemingly no regard to the emotional and financial expenditure associated with delivering results and profits. You have heard the saying "Business never sleeps" and "Time waits for no one." Therefore, it is imperative that we know all the time associated drivers so we can have in place a proactive approach to achieving our objectives rather than the ever so common high stress reactionary approach.

This proactive approach and identifying all the time drivers also allow us to be better prepared when reactionary is necessary due to events that actually require quick responses.

Example of Time Drivers on an Assessment List:

Time Drivers
Major Upcoming Business Events
Seasonal Demand/ Industry Cycles (Busy/ Slow)
Real Estate/ Equipment Lease Expirations Future Required Purchases
Payroll/ Tax Deadlines
Accounts Receivables/ Payables Timing
Sr. Leadership/ Employee Retirement
Product Delivery Lifecycles
Tools Maintenance Schedules/ Lifespan
Time Sensitive Contracts
Hours of Operation/ Increased Shifts

Fourth (T) Treasure, cash money – right? Yes, but a person and company possess vast amounts of wealth outside the conventional monetary definition. People have unique life experiences, perspective, a special skill or gift, a family heirloom, fond memories, future dreams and the deepest treasure of all, loving relationships. For companies, their people (Talent) top the list, then core values, brand, reputation, market share, proprietary and intellectual property, patents, unique ways of delivering goods and services and everything captured in financials including real estate, the place where your Talent delivers your vision to your clients (separate topic book in and of itself).

Example of Treasure on an Assessment List:

	Treasure
	Entire Organization Team (Custodian to CEO)
	Family/ Employee Owned/ Operated
	Company Brand/ Unique Logo/ Identity
	Market Share/ Reputation/ Client Loyalty
	Seen as Business/ Local Community Leader
	Patented Process for Delivering Goods/ Service
	Real Estate Premier Location/ Long-term Leases
	Owned Equipment/ Inventory
	Pref./ Best Price Supplier Vendor - Contracts
	Financial - Strong Balance Sheet

See next page.

Illustration that puts it all together:

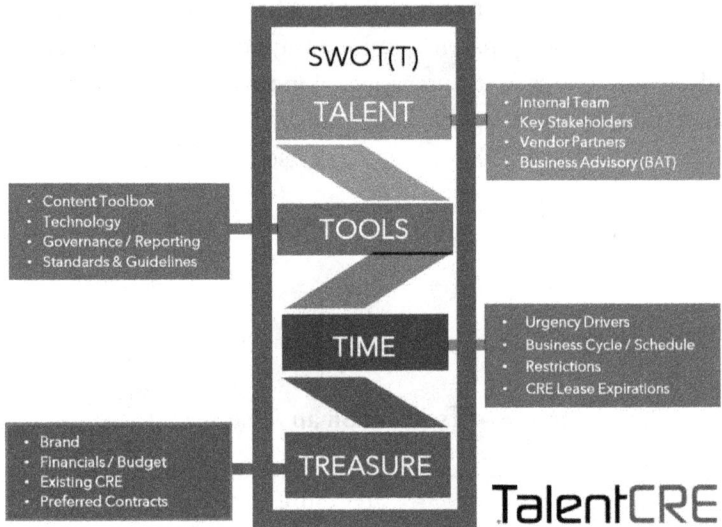

TCRE 4Ts™ Methodology

SWOT(T)

TALENT
- Internal Team
- Key Stakeholders
- Vendor Partners
- Business Advisory (BAT)

TOOLS
- Content Toolbox
- Technology
- Governance / Reporting
- Standards & Guidelines

TIME
- Urgency Drivers
- Business Cycle / Schedule
- Restrictions
- CRE Lease Expirations

TREASURE
- Brand
- Financials / Budget
- Existing CRE
- Preferred Contracts

TalentCRE

Now at this point you might be wondering what the **TCRE** stands for other than possibly the obvious abbreviation for TalentCRE, which it is, but it also is an acronym for our core values and guiding principles in everything we strive to be.

Transparency – 100% Visibility, Good and Bad.

Consideration – For Everyone and Every Situation.

Results – Focused.

Excellence – Always Striving to Achieve and Deliver.

7

2

Foundational Goals (FG's)

As we start to write this key chapter on how to achieve your goal's we are exactly 18 days removed from our TalentCRE 2020 Fourth quarter annual review meeting and nine days into 2021. The timing could not be better for us since this is the general timing most people and media are focused on the year that was and the next year that will be. We love this time of year because we can reminisce over all our victories and more importantly analyze our missteps and areas where we did not achieve what we set out to do.

Now it has been our experience and every other successful person we know of, that to get the most out of our lives you need to have a proven system or framework in place combined with faithful optimism. This system must be concise and in the proper sequence (priority) that captures your definition of an extraordinary life. Remember you get to decide your life's success measures, no one else.

The system we utilize that has had a profound impact and has changed our lives consists of four specific focus categories: **Health** - spiritual, mental, emotional and physical, **Family & Friends** – relationships, **Vocation** - what you were born to do and **Financial**. The sequence is paramount, for instance without personal health/self-care you will not possess the spiritual enlightened focused energy required to participate positively in all of life's wonderful experiences or worse your quality of life is diminished and possibly even cut short.

They all build on each other with financial purposefully left to last, because as you will learn if you have not already, no amount of money or material things will mean anything if you do not possess the first two, and when you add the third Vocation, you will have achieved a truly extraordinary life where Financial rewards will take care of itself (with simple philosophy/ discipline).

A great analogy for this is a Piña Colada 3 Layer Cake, where the cake represents Health, the filling is Family & Friends, the frosting is Vocation and the cherry on top is Financial.

See how insignificant the Cherry on top is and how unnecessary it is for an absolutely delicious, fully satisfying experience.

Now let's create your favorite cake!

FG's Action Items (AI's):

Some examples/ ideas only to get you started in the right direction, they should be specific and measurable, consist of short-term/ long-term and be reviewed daily, refined when necessary and replaced when successfully achieved or when other priority areas of focus reveal themselves. Remember you get to decide as well as having a proverbial clean slate to capture what is most important to you.

FG Examples/ Ideas List:

Health	Family & Friends	Vocation	Financial
Devote at least 20mins a day to Spiritual/ Emotional Growth	Create a Loving/ Respectful/ Safe/ Fun Home	Be the Top Project Manager in my field delivering complex projects across the Globe	Be Purposeful w/ my $, 10% Non-Profits/ 18% Save-Invest/ 72% Living
Eat 2 Bright Colored Vegetables a day	One Date a Month w/ Spouse/ Children	Attend Prof. Success Workshop	Develop Budget/ Lower My Expenses
Do 1 Physical Activity a day Even if it is just a Walk or Personal Chores	Take Friendship Adventure Vacation to Colorado	Join Community Outreach Program to use my Prof. Skills to Help	Pay Down Credit Card Balances to < 30% of Total Available Credit
Schedule Annual Health Checkups/ GO!	Find & Adopt a New Dog that Needs a Home	Identify/ Develop One New Skill this year	Spend 2hrs a week on Learning about Investing

See next page.

10

Brainstorm Notes:

AI's My Foundational Goals (2-4 max per category):

Category	GOAL/ (Specific & Measurable)
Health	
Health	
Health	
Health	
Family & Friends	
Family & Friends	
Family & Friends	
Family & Friends	
Vocation	
Vocation	
Vocation	
Vocation	
Financial	
Financial	
Financial	
Financial	

3

Your Brand, Inc.

The days of working Twenty-Five to Forty years for the same company with a cushy pension and a beautiful gold watch retirement party are over, and for most of you reading this, you never knew such a thing existed (which is an advantage). In the current marketplace you are an entity onto yourself, a freelancer who will have multiple roles with varied responsibilities. Therefore, it is imperative that you develop and continue to nurture a personal brand that highlights exactly how you want to be seen in the court of public opinion, which in today's global economy is always in session.

When you start developing or refining your public image the best course of action is to identify someone you respect in your field that has already achieved what you want to project. Then begin researching and modeling exactly what they have in place while remembering to capture your unique personality, experience and subject matter expertise. A word of caution when selecting who you want to model your desired public image, make sure you reconcile against all four categories of your FG's and it is aligned, more importantly not in conflict. This will ensure you capture the true representation of who you are and the extraordinary life you want to live and not just a cookie cutter replica.

Now that you have your FG's solidified and public image defined, it is time to finalize your personal brand and begin to Devise your Destiny. Simply put, you must know where you are going to successfully arrive at your destination. Armed with your FG's you can identify opportunities, roles, relationships and make purposeful choices to pursue and successfully achieve whatever you set your sights on. Setting your sights can take on many forms, in mind only (not recommended), writing down in a journal, notes strategically placed around where you will see them, photos, screensaver images or be in the form of a vision board (physical or digital). Whichever form you choose, please make sure your goals are memorialized, visible, reviewed daily and most importantly talked about and revealed to the world. Do not keep it a secret, tell your story, be the authentic you so the universe can conspire to put the right people and situations in your life for you to achieve an extraordinary life.

> *"You are always one conversation and*
> *decision away from changing your life.*
> *Make a choice, tell your story and*
> *be the authentic you."*

AI's Devising Destiny:

Remember your brand encompasses who you are personally and professionally, this is what differentiates you from everyone else and gives you a competitive advantage. Here are two tools that we have had great success in helping people devise their professional destiny. We have also included a brief success story and our TLTCRE New Opportunity Key Decision (KD) template that utilizes the TCRE 4Ts Methodology and highlights a personal/ professional cross functional application.

See next page.

TalentCRE

Future Pursuit

#	Questions
1	Timing: Immediate - 120 days
2	Time Horizon Duration: New Role 1-3-5yrs.
3	Region: US only or Global Opportunities, % of Travel and Willingness to Relocate?
4	Preferred Industries Sector: At least 3 Targets.
5	List of Transferable Skills / Assessments.
6	List of Strengths (highlight what you are happiest doing) / Value Add - Success examples.
7	Your Current Brand / Mission Story.
8	Target Roles for each Target Industry (wide net).
9	Target Companies.
10	Any additional information you believe is important.
11	Future Brand / Mission Story.

Due Diligence Questionnaire

Responses

Your definition aligned w/ FG's.

TalentCRE

TalentCRE

Week of	Activity
Sep 9	Finalize Foundational Goals (FG's)
Sep 16	Complete Due Diligence Questionnaire
Sep 16	Review / Revise / Finalize Due Diligence Questionnaire
Sep 16	Revise CV Focused on Value & Quantifiable Results
Sep 23	Review current brand in marketplace (Linkedin, assoc, affiliations, images, google, etc...)
Sep 23	Finalize CV, Start to identify Pursuit List w/ Roles / Companies / Sectors
Sep 23	Revise & Finalize Brand inline w/ Goals & Pursuit
Sep 30	Finalize Pursuit Targets / Start Active Contacts Networking - WK template
Oct 7	Active Pursuit w/ Network Pathways *Refine pursuit list w/ status update
Oct 14 & Oct 21	Active Pursuit w/ Network Pathways * Set-Take meets / refine pursuit list w/ status update
Oct 28 & Nov 4/11	Negotiate Short list Offers by Roles / Companies / Sectors **Exit Strategy 3-5-8yr Focus
Nov 18 & Nov 25	Secure Written & Executed New Role Contract w/ a minimum of 3-4wks break
Dec 9 & Dec 16	Give Notice Mon Dec 9th-Last Day 20th, **Victory Tour
Dec 23 & Dec 30	Holiday Break Celebrate Family / Friends / Victories
Jan 6	Start New Role

Key Activity Schedule 90

Status	Notes

TalentCRE

TLTCRE Team Member Brief Success Story

My current project was nearing completion and as the last major capital expenditure for the company for the foreseeable future, the pipeline for projects at scale was small. Also, having completed a complex project and knowing I have a growing family at home, there was a desire to move up in role, responsibility and income. With no desirable future with the current organization, I wanted to make a move. Instead of blindly putting out resumes or even contacting my network (at first) – I utilized the above process to identify certain aspects of the next role that I wanted, where and who I needed to be to land that interview and role.

My son was going to be born in late June, early July with a follow-on few weeks of parental leave through the summer into late summer, early fall. This timeline coincided with the finishing touches of a major project and would be the best time to complete my portion of the project and start something new.

In May, one month before my son was born, I completed the Due Diligence Questionnaire and reviewed with the assistance of my mentor. The exercise helped outline the timeline, the region and ideal companies. The exercise also made me rethink who I wanted to project and what my current resume said I was and who I really thought I was. The two were not exactly aligned. After much editing, refinement and sequencing of activities, the resume fully captured who I was and portrayed my responsibilities and accomplishments in a time sequential manner – A Day in the Life – that gave the reader a better sense of who I was and what I did.

After completing the questions, refining my resume and any external websites including LinkedIn, it was time to implement the key activity schedule. A side note – trust the process. Within a few weeks of putting the refined resume – based on my foundational goals and the questionnaire – I was experiencing a lot of interviews. And in those interviews, because the resume was time sequenced, it was easy to talk about and discuss in a coherent manner to the interviewer as sometimes, we all get to talking all over the place instead of answering the question.

A role was offered, salaries negotiated and critically, a start date a few weeks after my last day. Having a break to mentally transition from one role to the next – regardless of if in the same industry – is critical as each role in different companies is different. Give yourself that break, enjoy the time with family and friends and hit the ground running, refreshed and ready to provide extensive value.

See next page

TCRE 4Ts Cross Functional Application:

TalentCRE   New Oppty (KD) Key Decision Template

TLTCRE Network Member: Name   **Sr. TCRE Member:** Name

Date/Time: Month 00th, 2021 / 00:00pm est.

Executive Summary

Brief description Role / Company / Core values 1st Impressions / Overall -

TCRE 4Ts Due Diligence:

1. **Talent**
   a. Assessment List/ Notes -
2. **Tools**
   a. Assessment List/ Notes -
3. **Time**
   a. Assessment List/ Notes -
4. **Treasure**
   a. Assessment List/ Notes –

Foundational Goals (FG's) Alignment (at least 2)

1. **Health**
   a. Y/N – 1st Priority
   b. Y/N – 2nd Priority

2. **Family & Friendships**
   a. Y/N – 1st Priority
   b. Y/N – 2nd Priority

3. **Vocation**
   a. Y/N – 1st Priority
   b. Y/N – 2nd Priority

4. **Financial**
   a. Y/N – 1st Priority
   b. Y/N – 2nd Priority

TCRE 4Ts Final Key Decision

1. **Not Aligned w/ FG's multiple No's *No-Go**

   a. Why stmt. If No-Go Professionally/ Respectfully decline offer

2. **Aligned w/ FG's Yes *Go -Terms All Memorialized in Agreement **No Verbal**

   a. **Talent** – Clearly defined role w/ responsibility / accountability
      i. Details
   b. **Tools** – Necessary to perform role, Company Supplied/ Paid
      i. Details
   c. **Time** – Duration / Daily Commitment / Advancement / Exit strategy
      i. Details
   d. **Treasure** – Total Compensation
      i. Base Salary -
      ii. Performance Bonus -
      iii. Expenses Reimbursed w/ agreed cadence –
      iv. PTO –
      v. Benefits –
      vi. Other Measurable Comp -

4

Rules of the Road

Knowing how to navigate and setting yourself up on a path for success can be challenging without establishing clear expectations for yourself and others. You need best practices and policies to follow that will get you from point A to Z and back again, all the while preserving your sanity in this chaotic world that surrounds us all.

At TalentCRE we have taken a Rules of the Road approach that captures five key areas: values, professional conduct, work from home (WFH) including office environment, meetings and technology best practices. As you will see highlighted below, we have also incorporated some tricks of the trade from our professional services business that can be refined and utilized across any type of business as well as be applied to our personal lives (it is all intertwined).

Values

Your values inform your thoughts, words and actions. The world you experience is a direct result of the actions based on your values. There are two categories of values that will go into forming your overall core values: 1) Foundational Values, that capture what is most important to you personally or to your organization and 2) Service Professional Values that guide how you deal, specifically in your chosen vocation. As you can imagine these lists can become quite exhaustive especially when you consider everyone's unique life experiences and personal beliefs on what is important.

See next page.

Our Best Practice Values Shortlist:

Foundational Values		Service Professional Values
Authentic		Actively Engaged (Listen)
Balanced		Business Owner Oriented
Ethical		Committed to Overall Success
Fair		Excellence with Attention to Detail
Honest		Faithful and Realistically Optimistic
Integrity		Generous and Give More than you Receive
Loyal		Open Minded and Willing to Compromise
Optimistic		Organized and Prepared
Respectful		Results Focused
Trustworthy		Transparent with no Hidden Agendas

AI's My Values List:

Foundational Values		Professional Values

Professional Conduct

As a person and a successful professional you should be guided by your set of core values, knowing who you are, what is important to you and how you want to go about sharing what you have to offer with the world. A big part of getting to reveal who we are in our day to day lives is personal appearance, whether we like it or not, personal appearance plays an integral part in how we are perceived and received by the people we interact with.

We are not talking about looks, everyone is beautiful in their own unique way, we are talking about basic hygiene, cleanliness and choice of activity specific clothing and accessories. It is very important to let everyone know outwardly that you care about yourself and you have the confidence to show your unique self that projects Your Brand, Inc.

Best practice is to dress for your clients/ audience. Dress codes are based on working conditions and the effect your appearance will have on business relationships with other employees, people from other companies and the public. Standard dress should always be "business appropriate." This means different attire may be required based on your location, role and responsibilities. Use your best judgment combined with your right person Talent attributes highlighted in the TCRE 4Ts (ref. pg. 1) and you will be received positively on point.

Another integral part to professional conduct is maintaining and continuing to increase your industry knowledge and to participate in targeted training and activities that will enhance your chosen vocation. This will enable you to be apprised of new innovations, current trends and to keep your skills honed delivering creative solutions as well as ensuring you become a subject matter expert.

Best practice is to commit at least two hours a week to Your Brand, Inc., this can be formal training, informal self-directed training and research, personal development, networking and any source of focused engagement that will help you grow and broaden your knowledge base and connectivity to your industry. We have highlighted below some areas of focus from our Professional Services Industry that our team utilizes and that can be refined to your specific needs.

Our Best Practice List:

TalentCRE Methodologies	Continuing Education & Training
TCRE 4Ts Applications	Bachelors & Graduate Degree
TCRE Toolbox	Arch/ PE/ Real Estate/ MBA
TCRE PRISM Delivery	Public Speaking/ Presenting
TCRE 4Ts SWOT(T)	CAD/ Excel/ PPT/ Power BI
DART Program	Portfolio/ Workplace Strategy
Mentorship	Reading/ Online Content
Licenses & Certifications	**Memberships & Networking**
Architect (NCARB)	Non-Profit & Prof. Affiliations
Professional Engineer (PE)	Chamber of Commerce
Real Estate – Sales/ Broker	CoreNet/ NAR/ NAIOP
General Contractor GC/CM	BOMA/IFMA/NAHB/CCIM
PMP/CMCI/NCIDQ/CPM	Industry Events & Workshops
OSHA/ Green/ LEED/ Agile	Pick up the Phone * Say Hello

AI's Industry Knowledge Activities:

Remember value can be derived from a multitude of sources and increased knowledge can be found in the least obvious places, come up with your own prescription, be creative, stay energized and ensure your continued relevancy in the professional world.

Brainstorm Notes:

See next page.

AI's My Activities List (at least 2-4 per category):

Current/ New Methodologies	Continuing Education & Training
Licenses & Certifications	**Memberships & Networking**

Work from Home (WFH) - Remote & Office Environment

For some of us WFH and remote arrangements have always played a part in our day to day lives, for the rest WFH has only become a necessity since the recent global COVID-19 Pandemic. In any case the WFH – Remote trend is here to stay in some format either part of the week, part of the month or 100%. This arrangement can provide multiple benefits, decreased commuter costs and commute times, as well as an opportunity for a quiet, distraction-free working environment.

Similarly, in-office working offers perks such as a physical place to work, ability to socialize and the opportunity to collaborate with coworkers. In some cases, face to face communication and collaboration are vital and the need to be working side-by-side will only enhance your ability to service your clients and customers. Some of the best decisions and insights can come from hallway and cafeteria discussions, meeting new people and impromptu team meetings.

The subject of office hours and setting a schedule, in today's dynamic business environment and full access to technology and connectivity with seemingly endless demands on our time has become more important than ever to have and to set a workable schedule. Most of us still have a standard Monday through Friday work week generally falling between the time of 8am to 6pm, consisting of 8-9hr shifts with breaks for lunch and personal time. The remaining of us have all sorts of varied schedules depending on our chosen vocation, current situation, or preferred choice.

No matter what your situation you need to set a schedule that incorporates all your activities that are prioritized and aligned with your FG's. This is the only way you will be able to successfully manage your priorities and navigate the priorities of others. Since there are so many varied schedules with everyone's situation being unique and there are countless resources on making a successful schedule, we thought it best to just capture the one scheduling idea that has had the greatest impact for our teams.

Setting a definite start and stop time for working, that means when you are done working for the day you unplug, you do not check emails or respond, you do not make or answer phone calls. You do not perform any work outside of agreed upon working hours, unless of course it is an emergency (rarely the case), or you want to write down an idea or something you just do not want to forget before the next day. Make this key decision today and you will be amazed how much time you free up for all your other FG's activities.

See next page.

Our Best Practice Checklist:

WFH - Remote	Office Environment
Set a defined start and stop time for working hours that everyone knows	Set a defined start and stop time for working hours that everyone knows
Create a distraction free and quiet work area	Starts before you enter the building, be respectful, friendly and polite
Work surface and surrounding area should be clean and clutter free	Know and abide by all safe workplace protocols
Make sure you have full access to computer, phone and network applications	Get to know your office site including security and facilities staff - make a quick ref. contact list
Have a solid background ideally away from traffic areas	Work surface and surrounding area should be clean and clutter free
Be aware of background noise and utilize headset to control	Participate in team events and always clean up after yourself
WFH is not a replacement for dependent care, if required make sure they do not significantly detract from your ability to perform your duties during working hours	Emergency readiness, know your Security and Safety Captains, have a complete understanding and be ready to go on all emergency procedures and evacuation routes
Pay attention to personal appearance and be fully dressed, with the ability to participate in a video meeting	Show up on time (that means 5 mins before official start) in proper attire for days activity with the ability to participate in any meeting
When you have an illness and cannot adequately perform your duties take PTO, no work including answering calls or responding to emails	When you are under the weather or have an illness where you can adequately perform your duties WFH is the best option, be considerate of your office mates
Make sure you hydrate, take breaks and get up from your seat to stretch your legs in the fresh air	Make sure you hydrate, take breaks and get up from your seat to stretch your legs in the fresh air

Meetings

Every meeting formal or informal generally has a reason for that person requesting it, unless you are just getting together for fun, socializing, or catching up there should always be a definite reason. We used the word generally because as most of us have experienced a lot of the time we end up attending meetings where it seems we are just meeting to meet, no one has a clear understanding of why, or the why is vague with little assemblance of order and no clear objective or goal defined.

Now most of the time in our business we are fortunate enough to be running or facilitating meetings, ensuring there is a focused agenda with a clear objective and most importantly having an attendee list of people necessary to participate in achieving our collective goal. Remember time is everyone's most precious commodity, no matter if you are running or requested to attend a meeting you need to utilize best practices to ensure you are making the best use of everyone's time.

See next page.

Our Best Practice List:

Meetings - Best Practices
Have a clearly defined agenda on meeting invite.
When invited to a meeting with no agenda, tentatively accept meeting requesting agenda, if not supplied respectfully decline meeting.
Durations should be ½-1 hour with tight agendas and have takeaway action items.
Maximum meetings per day no more than 4hrs in an 8–10-hour business day.
Total meeting attendance a week no more than 12-15hrs in a 45–50-hour work week unless you are participating in work sessions or special events.
Utilize reporting governance and meeting schedule cadence to avoid unnecessary meetings, if no required action items, send detailed status updates only.
Recurring Client meetings set for Tues-Thurs between 10am and 4pm during a standard Mon-Fri work week.
Establish a midpoint to your day with no recurring meetings, a 1hr break is required to maintain energy and focus (12-1pm works for most).
As the Subject Matter Expert (SME), you have the expertise. Manage from a place of authority, dictate the tone and value your expertise as a strategic and tactical partner.
Attendee list: Only invite key participants, no client sub-contractor team combined meetings, you are the Owner and must establish and maintain authority to provide clear direction on what is necessary to achieve objectives.
Try to avoid one-off client Key D (Decision) meetings, having a supporting team member present ensures dual control and the availability of witness if required.
Follow up Key D with Email (EM) confirmation, memorialize in Client/ Project mailbox, this establishes permanent record with no revisionary history.
Know your audience – Client/ Customer/ Contractor/ Vendor and adjust accordingly, you want to make sure content and delivery is well received.
Leverage Technology Platform - Audio/ Visual tools (MSFT 365, Google Workspace, Salesforce Customer 360, Oracle NetSuite, Zoom, etc..).
At beginning of multi-participant meetings keep conversation light/ appropriate especially when waiting for other participants and do not speak about other clients.
When presenting material or sharing your screen make sure all confidential or other non-relevant content is closed and not visible to the group.
Meeting notes should be sent/ published within 24hrs.
Celebrate Key Accomplishments & Victories no matter how small.
Keep Perspective, Be the Authentic You & Always end on Positive.

Technologies Best Practices

Technology has become an integral part in our everyday lives, just about everyone has access to a computer, laptop or a hand-held, super-computer on them at all times (smart phone). It is hard to imagine life without these inventive productivity tools and all the incredible technology software they possess.

Whether it is MSFT 365, Google Workspace, Salesforce Customer 360, Oracle NetSuite, etc. – they all have their own unique offerings and benefits while also sharing similar attributes; constantly changing, refining existing platforms and inventing new. Even though this dynamic situation exist we can still utilize some best practices to help us be more efficient and secure. Here is our list, we are sure you have some of your own you can add.

See next page.

Our Best Practice List:

Technology - Best Practices
Keep all equipment/ accessories in one designated place including all chargers and when required to be mobile have an organized carrying case that fits everything.
Utilize webcam cover to avoid not being visible when not participating in video call.
Always use secure Wi-Fi and make use of Virtual Private Network (VPN).
Create Strong Passwords with at least 8-10 characters example: !UP3lower9
Lock computer and mobile phone whenever you are not in front of or leave your work area, including WFH.
Set up voicemail on Mobile Phone with short personal message and adjust message when out on PTO, so people know you are out and when to expect a return call.
Set up/ Load Email on Mobile Phone ** Check at least 2x daily during work hours.
Have a 'System' for organizing/ prioritizing email, set up rules to increase efficiency and utilize delay delivery to align with agreed upon business hours.
Email Signature Line should have at minimum: Closing Salutation, Name, tel. #, EM.
Color code calendar with key categories for quick reference identification and delineation from different types of scheduled activities.
Schedule recurring task work meeting times and unplug when performing task work.
Email subject lines should be concise and content should only cover one related topic, not multiple unrelated. Start new threads and avoid continuous run-on emails.
When writing an email try to capture all or at least the most important content in the paragraph viewable size of standard email view, best chance of getting attention.
In Business communications – no emoji's/text short-hand (☒, lol, ur, 2/to).
Email- Avoid replying all, reply only to Key participants (KP) until solution/ resolution is achieved. Especially with Clients unless KP, be considerate of everyone's inbox.
Email response time 24hr maximum, even if you do not have an answer yet, let them know you are working on it with a clear expectation of when you will complete.
When out on PTO identify backup resource & set up OOO message (email/ phone) with backup resource contact.
Naming convention for saving files: Date (YYMMDD) – Your Initials -Title -Subject, for example 210225-WK_TalentCRE_Client_ProjectMeetingMinutes.
If you modify/ update any file, update the file name with version number and your initials after the date. For example, if I noticed something wrong with Client Project Meeting Minutes and made an update, the format would follow: 210225v2-PS_TalentCRE_Client_ProjectMeetingMinutes.
No Phone Snubbing (Phubbing) when you are with clients, engaged in active conversation or participating in meetings. If you must look at phone, say excuse me, check quickly and close to lock screen.

5

Business Development

The most important determining factor on whether your business will be successful outside of your Talent and your unique offering is business development. How you develop and implement your marketing plan, overall go to market strategy and sales content. How you target clients, advertise and which mediums you choose to do so, and the sales process used for closing contracts. Each of these subjects is an entire book onto itself which other Authors have already successfully tackled and are readily available.

For our purposes we are going to focus on the **two crucial areas** we believe present the greatest challenges and if not done correctly can waste precious time as well as not allow you to establish the trust required to differentiate your value proposition on getting to your desired result - a closed sale/ contract.

The **first** is getting to the Key Decision Maker or the individual that actually has the authority to say yes and more importantly the authority to commit their funds to pay for your product or services. You can waste endless hours with time wasters or people who want free advice, free products and services or just do not have the ability to say yes in the way we need them to.

Now as you will see in the following TCRE 4Ts Methodology training session these people can play an important role to getting to the Key Decision Maker as well as provide invaluable information you can leverage when you get in front of the Key Decision Maker.

Pursuit Strategy – Get to Key Decision Maker (KDM)

Mindset - Think/ Act like a Business Owner and Leader

Goal – Get KDM Name

Perform - TCRE 4Ts SWOT(T)

o   **Talent**
- Outline the organization from the CEO down, identify Department Leads in Finance, Operations, Sales/ Marketing (these people will be easier to access).
- Outline their Competitors, Suppliers and Vendor Partners to understand their industry and who all the players are.
- Determine the SWOT(T) for each department regarding its Sr. Leadership talent to assist in identify gaps you can fill, weaknesses to supplement or strengths to compliment.

o   **Tools**
- Identify any proprietary tools they may be using or technology tools we already use.
- Identify any unique/ distinct delivery services.

o   **Time**
- In the research, know the businesses past and anticipate its needs for the future.
- Stay updated on news/ trends to determine overall business strategy in relation to the environment, future product/ service offering demand and customer profiles.
- Focus on innovations in product/ service delivery and impacts of season on cashflows, upcoming financial targets.

o   **Treasure**
- Know their top clients.
- Understand current CRE Portfolio and potential new sites.
- New contracts underway or visibility into future work.
- Strategic alliances you can access.

Training White Board Session

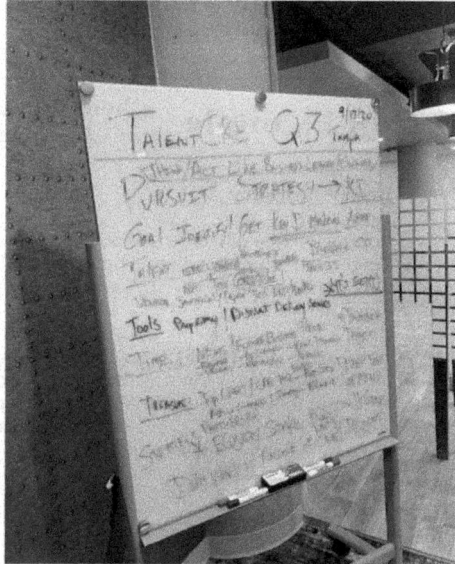

Key Takeaway: Perform full Due Diligence, approach the company as if you are going to take an Equity Stake or take over 100%; know the business; know the people; know their challenges and then when you get to the KDM, you can be positioned as a Strategic Partner peer providing a solution to their business needs and challenges with your unique service offering. Remember keep the 11 Step Success Plan front of mind and that we hire our clients.

TalentCRE

Second is the adoption of the Educational Sales approach, where you are committed to helping the client achieve their goals and business objectives rather than just selling a product or service. To do this, you must learn their business and have a clear understanding on the areas where they might not have all the facts and where you can bring added value. Once you have implemented/ completed the due diligence and have secured a date/ time with the Key Decision Maker, you can then utilize your subject matter expertise and your experience helping others through case stud-

Snapshot Example	Client Pursuit – Return to Office/ Change Mgmt.

Brief Summary

Completed due diligence on an IT firm New Client Pursuit Target and found out, in this time of COVID-19, that they have a myriad of long-term/ short-term leases in US East Coast major cities.

In the news, it seems like these companies may be losing money on unused spaces as their people work from home but still want to keep a footprint for in-person collaboration and work on confidential/ proprietary products and services.

Challenges

Talent - Attrition of talent if WFH flexibility is not allowed/ capable along with collaborative spaces.

Tools - Some technology can only be done on-site.

Time - Speed to market is critical at the IT firm, leases are short-term and long-term.

Treasure - Current space utilization is low; losing money with leased spaces (rent, utilities, Support Personnel), Brand may be compromised if unable to attract/ retain the best talent.

Results & Lessons Learned

Treasure - Renegotiate lease terms, include in marketing materials and HR, WFH flexibility policies and support including day care at office.

ies, lessons learned and proven solutions that you will highlight in their specific Day in the Life scenario (see snapshot example).

This approach creates an environment of trust and solidifies your value as an advisor/ strategic partner in achieving their goals. If done properly your product or service will sell itself, all you will have to do is formalize it in a mutually equitable transaction and close the sale. Remember their success is your success.

TCRE MD - Sierra   May 1, 2020

<u>Day In the Life</u>

Organization RTO/ Employee Change Mgmt.

TCRE 4Ts SWOT(T) – Assessment/ Options/ Best Path Forward.

Start - Review of Leases and space configuration, notify workforce that leadership is aware of the challenges and a program is underway to address these challenges.

Design - Engage SME to design space configuration to accommodate requirements and brokers to determine impacts. Engage workforce in design with surveys/ meetings to bring in their ideas and spur employee support and participation.

Build - Implement space designs and lease negotiations/ send regular updates to workforce of new changes and how to engage with updated spaces and technology.

Finish - Complete space configuration; Close negotiations; Reoccupy. Provide training to workforce on new upgrades/ changes; make available SME for training/ information.

Survey & Iteration - Gain feedback from workforce through surveys, focus groups and individual talks. Provide celebrations and recognition of hard work and highlight successes with future programs to come.

Result – Successful Safe Return to Office

TalentCRE

6

Closing the Sale/ Contracts

If you have done everything right up to this point and you are in front of the Key Decision Maker, how do you go about achieving the most important and for many, the most elusive aspect in determining whether your endeavors will be successful or not - closing the sale. Before we reveal that, we must cover the two biggest mistakes people make when trying to win a sale. Take a moment and see if you can guess what these mistakes could be and why they are so detrimental in achieving your desired result – a closed sale/ contract.

Your Guess:

o   Mistake #1

o   Mistake #2

Answers on the next page.

Mistake #1

Never Asking for The Sale!

It is hard to believe but most people who are not successful in closing a sale never ask for what they came to get – a sale. Whether they get lost in the process, do not know when to bring up (spoiler alert it is not at the end), plain forget, fear of getting a no, believe it will somehow miraculously just take care of itself or even worse not know the value they are providing to have the confidence to ask for it. Whatever the reason, you must never make this mistake (bad habit) again, especially since it is so easy to change and when you do, your closing ratio will begin to soar.

Remember in Your Brand, Inc. do not keep your intentions a secret, the same applies here, let people know what you want and how much you are willing to give to achieve it. You will be pleasantly surprised on how much you will receive in return.

Mistake #2

Not Listening!

This one crosses all aspects of our lives and everyone can relate to, how many times has your voice not been heard, silenced for some reason, or not been able to get the other person to listen to what you were trying to convey. Notice we said listen and not hearing, they are distinctly different.

We are surrounded by all sorts of sounds unpleasant and pleasant, and unless you are hearing impaired, hearing is constant, passive and achieved through physical vibrations entering the ear (nothing required on your part). In contrast listening is performed by the brain, it is selective, active and to do well, takes focus, concentration and a genuine interest in what is being expressed.

Not listening as pertains to closing the sale can have a deep impact on you being successful during the entire educational sales process. If not made a priority you could miss a key element to their business, you may forget to address relevant concerns, or potentially try selling them something they do not need or worse providing them with a sub par product that does not add value (bad news travels fast). It is also imperative to utilize focused listening when you run into resistance, when they do not want to say yes or buy. If you listen closely people tell you what they want, we like to call it their hidden buy trigger (what is most important to them).

Listen to exactly what they are saying and how they are saying it, address their problems and concerns with pinpoint accuracy on solving their problems and bringing added value to them and their organization. Identify their buy trigger, listen to what others are not and you will be able to pivot and home in on exactly what it will take to win the sale.

Now let us show you the detailed steps with the precise sequence of actions to conducting an educational closing focused sales meeting/ presentation that will result in achieving the elusive closed sale. One caveat, they must truly be a potential client that can benefit from what you are offering. So, prior to setting any meeting you must first ask yourself:

What product/ service do we have that the client needs?

Why do they need our product/ service?

Why do they need our product/ service today (really-yesterday)?

Armed with these answers you can go into the sales presentation with complete confidence that what you have to offer will bring them great value. Now how do you translate that confidence and value proposition into a closed sale? We follow a proven systematic Eleven Step Success Plan that starts from the time we arrive and when everything goes right has us leaving with a signed contract and new professional friendship.

TCRE Sales Presentation – 11 Step Success Plan

Step 1: Warm up – Familiarity **Anything but Business

When you arrive at their location or in today's world virtually, look for something that is personally significant to them or something you share a common interest. Warmly introduce yourself and immediately start talking about that aspect of their life, casual, relaxed and as if you are starting a new friendship - you are. Remember people like to do business with people they like and who they are familiar.

Step 2: Determine Client Needs
    – Questions & Answers **Listen

Start with thanking them for meeting with you, briefly state the product/ service you have that will meet their needs and then ask how can I help? Listen actively, take notes on their challenges and continue asking questions and getting answers until you are absolutely clear on where you can provide value.

Step 3: Company Story – Why they called you and your personal reason why you are with the company

Give them a succinct description of your Company, brand, history, reputation, etc. and then tell your personal story on why you choose to be with this particular Company and what separates them from the pack (hint – talent/ core values). Remember they have a choice when choosing who they want to do business with and by you revealing your reasons shows that you believe in your company and you know that it is the right type of organization that can bring them value.

Step 4: Define Meeting Objective – Introduce Products/ Services offered, make it clear they will get a firm price and that you are going to do business today (less than halfway in and already asking for the sale)

This is when the meeting takes a more focused structured approach from the client's perspective, you are clearly defining what you have to offer, your product value will be evident and they will get favorable terms/ pricing and it is your intention that you want to win their business today.

Step 5: Detail Service Platform
   – Personalize to Individual/ Client

Lay out exactly how you are going to deliver your product to them, combination of narrative and illustrations. Show them the talent/ workflow/ moving parts, reassure them that you know how to deliver from start to finish and that you have command and control over the entire process ensuring they will receive positive results.

Step 6: Detail Products Offered
   – Personalize to Individual/ Client

Show them specific product offerings, ideally three options tailored to their needs, combination of narrative and illustrations. Highlight your unique value proposition and potential additional products or services you can supply if, and when there is a future need.

Step 7: Product Delivery Platform
   – Circle of Risk Diagram/ Story

Here is where you present the call to action, outlining the risks and danger of negative cascading events that could happen if they do not go with you for their product needs. Tell through an actual story of start to finish critical events during the product delivery process where other providers fell short or where things went seriously wrong that can be avoided by going with you.

Step 8: Present Price to Client
      – Only answer questions, not responses or statements

Now ask for the sale, give them the detailed price and let them know it would be a privilege to have them as a client. Then here is where the real intestinal fortitude comes into play, only answer questions for clarification on what you have presented, not responses or statements. With one exception being the response of NO, if this happens and it will, you will then have to implement the 3x rule.

The 3x Rule is what we use whenever we encounter someone not wanting what we have offered (saying no) or more importantly, not understanding the value our unique product or service will bring to them. So, to overcome the first no, we simply ask them what is it that they do not like about our offer? We then respond with detailed points addressing those concerns and doubling down on our unique value proposition and asking for the sale again.

At this time, we will most likely get a Yes, if for some reason we do not and get another no (2nd no), we then try a third time by employing the same strategy and restating point by point the value and how we have addressed every one of their concerns. Then we ask one final time for the sale. If they are truly in the market and we have demonstrated great value and their immediate need for our product, we will get a Yes and win the sale.

In some instances, you are going to get and must accept a 3rd no. When this occurs you better have a clear understanding of why you are leaving without winning the business, because without knowing the why they said no, you will never be able to receive the Victory of the loss or the no.

"Every Loss or Perceived Failure is an Opportunity to Learn How to Win and Succeed."

Step 9: Close Sale/ Sign Contracts – Once Signed
        **Stop Selling

You get the Yes. Now close it, make them commit by having them sign the contract, **Victory Contract Signed!**
Smile & Stop Selling.

Step 10: Cool Down – Assurances and Niceties

This is very important, when someone purchases something or commits a large sum of money the entire process for them can be a mixed bag of emotions. So now is the time for reassuring them they made the right choice, how much of a pleasure it was meeting with them and how you are going to be available for anything that might arise during your new professional relationship (friendship).

Step 11: Leave – Happy & Humble *Self-explanatory*

Goal – Closed Project Mgmt. Contract

Pre – Meet Answers:

○ **What Product/ Service do we have that Client Needs?**
  - After doing due diligence, the client needs project management services to lead the planning, design and new construction of a building.

○ **Why do they need our Product/ Service?**
  - They need our PM services – which is founded on the experience of our people, our results focused-ownership mentality, and our methodologies and tools – because their personnel are young and there is no one set of SOPs. The company needed our Project Management Services and Tools.

○ **Why do they need our Product/ Service Today (Yesterday)?**
  - This project is regulatory driven and a requirement by local government per tax incentives and needing completion in 24 months. The timing is now.

11 Step Success Plan (RFP Response & Presentation):

○ **Warm Up**
  - In the age of Zoom, Remote interviews may be more the case than not. During the setting up as people join, light conversation about a painting in the background of an interview warmed everyone up.

○ **Determine Client Needs**
  - As we opened our presentation, discussing the agenda and a brief introduction of the team and our services, we went directly into a Q/A sessions to determine what exactly was going on, the challenges the client was experiencing and how they saw the project play out. We listened, wrote down the challenges with the knowledge that we would address those specific challenges within the presentation – adding immediate value to their organizations and qualifying our abilities.

○ **TalentCRE Story**
  - After the Q/A session, we pause and say, "We'll talk about those challenges shortly, but just want to go into a little about ourselves, the team and why I'm part of it." After being at multiple staff augmentation CRE organizations, I decided to join TCRE where advisory/ strategic partnership were the focus. This allows me to act on the best interest of the client and provide CRE Excellence.

11 Step Success Plan (cont.):

○ **Define Meeting Objective**
- In this part, we discuss the overall services, products offered, our goal to win business and that at the end of the presentation, we'll discuss the rates, etc.

○ **Detail TCRE Service Platform**
- Following the above and based on the Q/A session, discussed our local expertise in the permitting process, our local footprint and network of vendors as well as our internal network of SMEs to ensure quality assurance of design and construction.

○ **Detail TCRE Products Offered/ Delivery Platform (combined due to flow)**
- As the presentation/ conversation continued and we describe how we can address permitting and knowledge of local vendors, we also sprinkle in our personal experiences with other organization – making sure to highlight the challenges of using local market resources with limited expertise and the impacts on budget, schedule and long-term relationships for future work.
- This back and forth creates an idea in the client that without us and our experience, they may experience the same thing. We can help them not have that happen.

○ **Present Price to Client**
- As we close the presentation, wrapping up the challenges, our services and the risk of not having us, we presented our rates – highlighting any preferred client discounts provided and the transparency of our profits and our charitable contributions.
- At this point, silence, we waited for questions – a few popped up but none that couldn't be answered. The key here was being transparent on the pricing and breaking down line items. There were a few comments, but we remained quiet – only answering questions, not adding to comments.

○ **Close Sale – Sign Contracts**
- A few days had passed where the client came back with clarifying questions but eventually awarded the contract to our team – signing and letting us begin.

○ **Cool Downs/ Leave (combined due to virtual)**
- Upcoming weekend talk and thank you notes were sent immediately after the presentation and after the award.

TalentCRE

TalentCRE

NEW CLIENT / BUSINESS PROTOCOL

Pre – Meet Answers

☐ **What Product / Service do we have that Client Needs?**

Answer:

☐ **Why do they need our Product / Service?**

Answer:

☐ **Why do they need our Product / Service Today (yesterday)?**

Answer:

Sales Presentation – 11 Step Success Plan

☐ **Warm Up:** Familiarity *Anything but Business.
☐ **Determine Client Needs:** Questions & Answers *Listen
☐ **TalentCRE Story:** Why they called you & Personal reason why you are with TalentCRE.
☐ **Define Meeting Objective:** Introduce TCRE, Products / Services offered **Make it clear they will get a firm price & you are going to do business today.
☐ **Detail TCRE Service Platform:** Personalize to Individual / Client.
☐ **Detail TCRE Products Offered:** Personalize to Individual / Client.
☐ **Product Delivery Platform:** Circle of Risk Diagram / Story *TalentCRE Network Team Identification & CRE Services.
☐ **Present Price to Client:** Only answer questions, not responses or statements.
☐ **Close Sale-Sign Contracts:** Once Signed **Stop Selling!
☐ **Cool Down:** Assurances & Niceties.
☐ **Leave:** Happy & Humble.

7

TCRE PRISM

Putting it all together, the TCRE PRISM, a simplified, results focused, proven integrated success model (PRISM - see illustration). Now some of you depending on your professional experience will notice familiar concepts that are captured, most obvious is our version of project management delivery that is embedded.

This is by design, first because it is based on a tried-and-true universal delivery method that has been used for centuries across all geographies and cultures to achieve successful outcomes, and second because in our decades of successfully building structures it has been made absolutely clear to us that without the proper foundational blocks in the right sequence you will not be able to build anything that will stand the test of time.

The other elements captured are a blend of our unique perspective, personal/ professional experience, intellectual property and who we are as an organization combined with just the right amount of important and relevant key activities in a systematic, continuous delivery loop that results in guaranteed success across multiple applications.

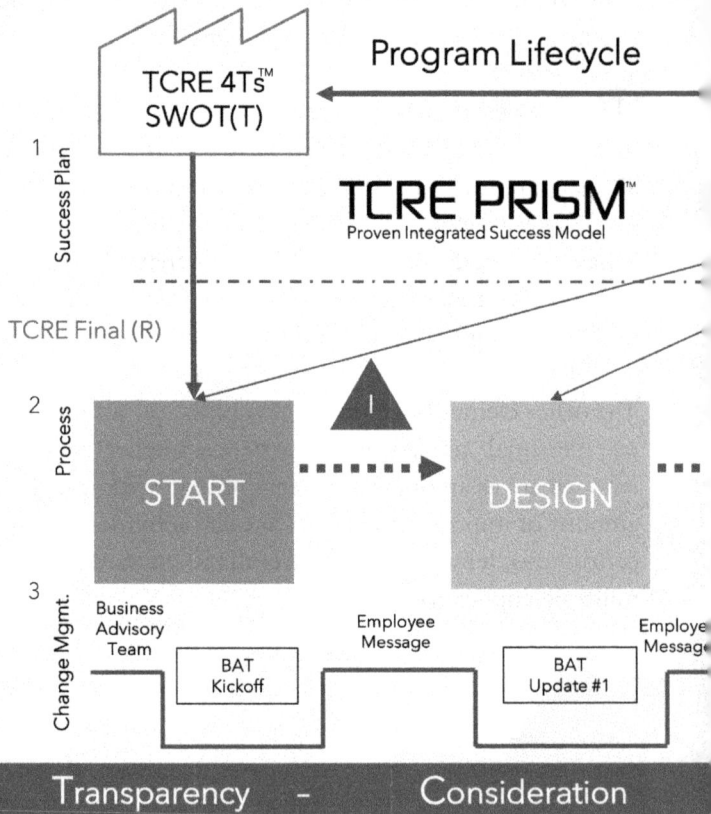

TalentCRE
An MWBE Commercial Real Estate Firm

Program Lifecycle

TCRE 4Ts™
SWOT(T)

TCRE PRISM™
Proven Integrated Success Model

1 Success Plan

TCRE Final (R)

2 Process

START

I

DESIGN

3 Change Mgmt.

Business Advisory Team		Employee Message		Employee Message
	BAT Kickoff		BAT Update #1	

Transparency – Consideration

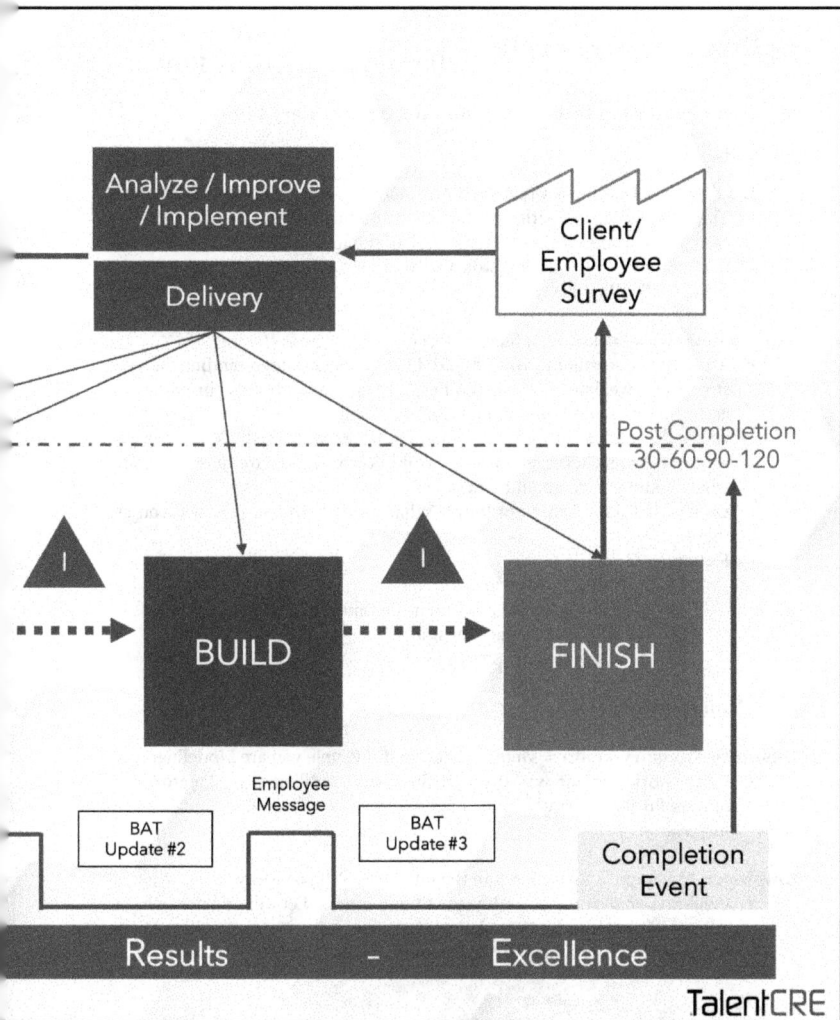

Analyze / Improve / Implement

Delivery

Client/ Employee Survey

Post Completion
30-60-90-120

BUILD

FINISH

Employee Message

BAT Update #2

BAT Update #3

Completion Event

Results - Excellence

TalentCRE

Goal – Implementation Framework for an Extraordinary Life

Success Plan:

o **TCRE 4Ts** = FG's Develop & Create Self Awareness/ Self Reflection/ Self Analysis
  - The process begins with an assessment of the current situation. In this case, its your life within the framework of the four foundational goals. How is your life going with regards to the four foundational goals? What is going well? What isn't?

o **TCRE Final (R)** = Locked FG's Memorialized
  - After the assessment, you should have a clear understanding of your strengths, weakness, opportunities, threats and trends in your life according to your foundational goals. Decide, according to your goals, where do you want to focus? What can be strengthened? What can you exploit now and leverage in your favor? What trends are happening and what should you do about them?
  - Lock your FG's – What are they? What needs help and how will you get there?
  - Example:
    - ❑   Health: Lose 25 lbs.
    - ❑   Family & Friends: Spend more time with Parents.
    - ❑   Vocation: Start new business.
    - ❑   Financial: Earn $75K this year.

Change Management:

o **Business Advisory Team** = Mentors/ Successful People you are Modeling.
  - While working your way through the goals – utilizing the Mentors and Successful people you're modeling – to give you feedback, guidance and inspiration.

o **Employee Message** = Releasing into the universe *Tell you Story.
  - Celebrate your victories with yourself and others. Let others know what is going well, but also let them know where you are struggling, what you are trying to do to over those struggles and how they can help.

Process:

- **Start** = Health FG's
  - As discussed in previous chapters, start with your Health FGs – because without breath or mental capacity, you can't do the other goals. Begin working your way through the goals – utilizing the Mentors and Successful people you're modeling – to give you feedback, guidance and inspiration.
  - Lose 25 lbs.
    - ❑ Set up exercise routine.
    - ❑ Join running group of successful runners.
- **Design** = Family & Friends FG's
  - Spend more time with Parents.
    - ❑ Set up lunch every Sunday.
    - ❑ Ask friends who have great relationships with parents what they do to stay connected.
- **Build** = Vocation FG's
  - Start a new Business.
    - ❑ Review personal finances and discuss risks with family.
    - ❑ Network with those who not only started a similar business but any business for experiences and lessons learned.
- **Finish** = Financial FG's
  - Earn $75K per year.
    - ❑ Increase skills in industry and salary negotiation.
    - ❑ Network with those in your industry a level or two above you to find out what they did.

Success Plan Review/ Update:

- **Employee Survey** = Self-Analysis / Measuring Results
  - Check in and be real with yourself. How are you doing? What's going well? What isn't? What are you going to do about it?
- **Analyze/ Improve/ Implement** = Refine/ Commit/ Continue/ Believe & Achieve
  - After the check-in, which can be the 4Ts Assessment again, revise your Process and implement whatever needs to be addressed.

TalentCRE

Brief Summary: In Q2 of 2020, XYZ Business requested an assessment and implementation plan to return to work during the COVID 19 crisis. The company specializes in information technology (IT) services and are supported by day to day operational/ admin services.

Goal – Safe Return to Work while maintaining business continuity/ profitability.

Success Plan:

o **TCRE 4Ts** = Business Assessment
  - A complete assessment of the business was conducted determined that they were strong in Talent, Tools and Treasure but weak with Time – as the company had planned to return to their office by Q4 2020 but being it was Q2, planning was already behind.

o **TCRE Final (R)** = 3 Options with a Final Recommend
  - Utilizing the assessment as a foundation, three options were created on how the company should position their real estate and return to work. Our company provided a recommendation for final approval by the client.

Change Management:

o **Business Advisory Team**
  - Continuous communication with Executive Sponsor and Lines of Business Leads.

o **Employee Message**
  - Distribution of newsletters, townhalls and furniture mockups for employee change management.

o **Post Completion**
  - Days during the lifecycle for events to occur.

Process (snapshot detail):

- **Start**
  - Kickoff & Goal Alignment.
  - Due Diligence/ Site-Visits.
  - Complete Speed Charter.
  - Lease Abstract.

- **Design**
  - Scope Definition.
  - Review / Approve SD's / DD's / CD's.
  - RFP's Vendors/ Award Contracts.
  - Lock Build (Scope/ Budget/ Schedule).

- **Build**
  - Assoc. Moves/ FFE Removal.
  - Demo/ Construction.
  - FFE Install.
  - Testing/ Commissioning.

- **Finish**
  - Punchlist Complete.
  - FM Handoff.
  - Occupy Move In.
  - Final Invoices/ Unconditional Lien Waiver.
  - Final Close Package.

Success Plan Review/ Update:

- **Employee Survey**
  - Asking the workforce how they are doing? How were the moves and/ or new equipment? Get feedback to address and plan for future projects.

- **Analyze/ Improve/ Implement**
  - With the feedback from the Executive Sponsor, Internal project teams and Workforce, refine the analysis, implementation and change management processes for future programs.

TalentCRE

8

TCRE 4Cs

It has been our experience that most problems and the source of majority of issues that arise in our professional endeavors as well as in our day-to-day personal lives can be solved by implementing a simple solution strategy that we have refined over the years to ensure a unified path forward, focused on results.

TCRE 4Cs

Communication – If we are not talking (all forms) there is absolutely no way for us to know or understand what is required of us to collectively succeed. When we start communicating effectively and have deep dialogue around all aspects of the ins outs of what is happening (forces internal and external), we can then start solutioning by means of the next C.

Collaboration - Everyone needs to work together in a positive respectful manner, leveraging their expertise and unique experience. Collectively we are better at problem solving and can be more effective, efficient and achieve at a far higher level than if we are working in silos or apart with competing agendas.

Consistency - Show up, day in and day out, as a known trusted commodity able to be counted on, committed to the team, process and the end goal.

Closeout – Finish everything you are responsible for. Every task you start, you track the progress and see it through to the end, ensuring that everything is completely done and nothing falls through the cracks.

simplification - Continuously identify ways to make things easier and less complicated. Focus on increased efficiencies that will lead to faster delivery and enhanced results.

"All happy families are alike; each unhappy family is unhappy in its own way."

- Tolstoy, Anna Karenina

The same thing can be said of teams. Great teams seem the same – typically showing similar characteristics. On the other hand, bad teams can be terrible in an infinite number of ways.

Example of Non-unified Team – Only one C missing:

The project to help this business Return to Work, upgrade their spaces and enable their people to get back to work in a hybrid fashion went well. The team **communicated** not just on a systemic "Kickoff" every week but used existing technology to ping each other when questions arose. In meetings, when difficult situations required problem solving, each team member rose to the occasion, **collaborated** and gave input and honest feedback to ensure the problem was analyzed from all angles and solutions were comprehensive. **Consistency** was the norm, there was never a time when someone did not show up as planned, or when called, did not respond – whether it was a full response or just, I will get back to you. The team knew we were there for each other when we called.

Unfortunately, at the end of the project through all the communication, collaboration and consistent engagement it was found that a key stakeholder who was responsible for the occupy event did not **closeout** an assigned task of securing the approval and additional required security to occupy. At the end, when all was great – the key element needed to host a celebratory turn over event was incomplete and the event had to be rescheduled.

The client was not happy. The project was difficult, the stakes were high, and to, at the last moment, not complete an item so simple, was disappointing to the overall project and could have been avoided.

A project hitting on all cylinders but ultimately unsuccessful in the eyes of the client and workforce due to a non-unified team. That situation may seem unfair as things were going well. The team may have deserved the benefit of the doubt given all their previous successes – but when you are committed to delivering service excellence, as a mentor of mine used to say,

"You can build a thousand bridges, but let one fall down and that's the one you're remembered for."

Same Example Unified Success – All 4Cs Engaged

Now take the above situation and simply incorporate this non-construction turn over key activity to the finished closeout checklist prior to the end. Making this one **simple** addition could have ensured that the elements required to host event would have been in place fully complete and on time - resulting in a successful project on all fronts. Not only would their goals be met, but they would be exceeded with a successful project by a unified team, resulting in client/ workforce satisfaction.

Bonus C

There is one more C word that is imperative to possess and the one common trait every successful person shares. Do you know what it is? Think of all the people you know that are successful no matter what their age, profession or endeavor they choose to take on. Got your list, what do they all have in common?

Your List:

Your Guess:

Answer on the next page.

Competitive!

To be successful you must be competitive and have a competitive spirit where you are 100% committed to Winning no matter what the obstacles or perceived competitor stands in your way. Notice we said perceived competitor not competitor or competition. This is because we believe whole heartedly that:

"The only Competition you have in Life, is to be the Best You."

If you are 100% committed to being your best in all your endeavors and they are aligned with your Foundational Goals, you can know with absolute certainty that you have already won the day and it is of no concern who or what entity stands on the other side in determining your success. Be your best and the Victories will follow.

9

Quick Reference Field Guide

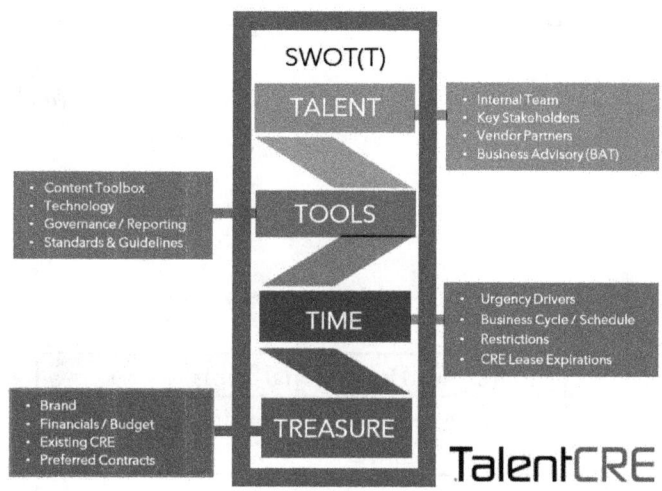

TCRE 4Ts™ Methodology

SWOT(T)

TALENT
- Internal Team
- Key Stakeholders
- Vendor Partners
- Business Advisory (BAT)

TOOLS
- Content Toolbox
- Technology
- Governance / Reporting
- Standards & Guidelines

TIME
- Urgency Drivers
- Business Cycle / Schedule
- Restrictions
- CRE Lease Expirations

TREASURE
- Brand
- Financials / Budget
- Existing CRE
- Preferred Contracts

TalentCRE

Talent Reference:

o   Disaster – Bernie Madoff

o   Success – Maya Angelou

"All my work, my life, everything I do is about survival, not just bare, awful, plodding survival, but survival with grace and faith. While one may encounter many defeats, one must not be defeated."

-Maya Angelou

Example of Tools on an Assessment List:

Professional Tools
Technology - Computers/ Smartphones Software/ Security
Manufacturing/ Logistics Platform
Diagnostic/ Testing Equipment
Personal Protection Equipment (PPE)
Specialty Machinery/ Vehicles
Operations Manuals/ Procedures
Marketing/ Advertising Content
Leads Source Lists/ Sales Scripts
Playbooks/ Project Mgmt. Processes
Workplace Standards/ Guidelines

Example of Time Drivers on an Assessment List:

Time Drivers
Major Upcoming Business Events
Seasonal Demand/ Industry Cycles (Busy/ Slow)
Real Estate/ Equipment Lease Expirations Future Required Purchases
Payroll/ Tax Deadlines
Accounts Receivables/ Payables Timing
Sr. Leadership/ Employee Retirement
Product Delivery Lifecycles
Tools Maintenance Schedules/ Lifespan
Time Sensitive Contracts
Hours of Operation/ Increased Shifts

Example of Treasure on an Assessment List:

Treasure
Entire Organization Team (Custodian to CEO)
Family/ Employee Owned/ Operated
Company Brand/ Unique Logo/ Identity
Market Share/ Reputation/ Client Loyalty
Seen as Business/ Local Community Leader
Patented Process for Delivering Goods/ Service
Real Estate Premier Location/ Long-term Leases
Owned Equipment/ Inventory
Pref./ Best Price Supplier Vendor - Contracts
Financial - Strong Balance Sheet

FG Examples/ Ideas List:

Health	Family & Friends	Vocation	Financial
Devote at least 20mins a day to Spiritual/ Emotional Growth	Create a Loving/ Respectful/ Safe/ Fun Home	Be the Top Project Manager in my field delivering complex projects across the Globe	Be Purposeful w/ my $, 10% Non-Profits/ 18% Save-Invest/ 72% Living
Eat 2 Bright Colored Vegetables a day	One Date a Month w/ Spouse/ Children	Attend Prof. Success Workshop	Develop Budget/ Lower My Expenses
Do 1 Physical Activity a day Even if it is just a Walk or Personal Chores	Take Friendship Adventure Vacation to Colorado	Join Community Outreach Program to use my Prof. Skills to Help	Pay Down Credit Card Balances to < 30% of Total Available Credit
Schedule Annual Health Checkups/ GO!	Find & Adopt a New Dog that Needs a Home	Identify/ Develop One New Skill this year	Spend 2hrs a week on Learning about Investing

FG's Priority

A great analogy for this is a Piña Colada 3 Layer Cake, where the cake represents Health, the filling is Family & Friends, the frosting is Vocation and the cherry on top is Financial.

See how insignificant the Cherry on top is and how unnecessary it is for an absolutely delicious, fully satisfying experience.

Your Brand, Inc.

"You are always one conversation and decision away from changing your life. Make a choice, tell your story and be the authentic you."

Devising Professional Destiny:

TalentCRE

Future Pursuit

#	Questions
1	Timing: Immediate - 120 days
2	Time Horizon Duration: New Role 1-3-5yrs.
3	Region: US only or Global Opportunities, % of Travel and Willingness to Relocate?
4	Preferred Industries Sector: At least 3 Targets.
5	List of Transferable Skills / Assessments.
6	List of Strengths (highlight what you are happiest doing) / Value Add - Success examples.
7	Your Current Brand / Mission Story.
8	Target Roles for each Target Industry (wide net).
9	Target Companies.
10	Any additional information you believe is important.
11	Future Brand / Mission Story.

Due Diligence Questionnaire

Responses

Your definition aligned w/ FG's.

TalentCRE

Devising Professional Destiny:

TalentCRE

Pursuit

Week of	Activity
Sep 9	Finalize Foundational Goals (FG's)
Sep 16	Complete Due Diligence Questionnaire
Sep 16	Review / Revise / Finalize Due Diligence Questionnaire
Sep 16	Revise CV Focused on Value & Quantifiable Results
Sep 23	Review current brand in marketplace (Linkedin, assoc, affiliations, images, google, etc...)
Sep 23	Finalize CV, Start to identify Pursuit List w/ Roles / Companies / Sectors
Sep 23	Revise & Finalize Brand inline w/ Goals & Pursuit
Sep 30	Finalize Pursuit Targets / Start Active Contacts Networking - WK template
Oct 7	Active Pursuit w/ Network Pathways *Refine pursuit list w/ status update
Oct 14 & Oct 21	Active Pursuit w/ Network Pathways * Set-Take meets / refine pursuit list w/ status update
Oct 28 & Nov 4/11	Negotiate Short list Offers by Roles / Companies / Sectors **Exit Strategy 3-5-8yr Focus
Nov 18 & Nov 25	Secure Written & Executed New Role Contract w/ a minimum of 3-4wks break
Dec 9 & Dec 16	Give Notice Mon Dec 9th-Last Day 20th, **Victory Tour
Dec 23 & Dec 30	Holiday Break Celebrate Family / Friends / Victories
Jan 6	Start New Role

Key Activity Schedule 90

Status	Notes

TalentCRE

TCRE 4Ts Cross Functional Application:

TalentCRE — New Oppty (KD) Key Decision Template

TLTCRE Network Member: Name **Sr. TCRE Member:** Name

Date/Time: Month 00th, 2021 / 00:00pm est.

Executive Summary

Brief description Role / Company / Core values 1st Impressions / Overall -

TCRE 4Ts Due Diligence:

1. **Talent**
   a. Assessment List/ Notes -
2. **Tools**
   a. Assessment List/ Notes -
3. **Time**
   a. Assessment List/ Notes -
4. **Treasure**
   a. Assessment List/ Notes –

Foundational Goals (FG's) Alignment (at least 2)

1. **Health**
   a. Y/N – 1st Priority
   b. Y/N – 2nd Priority

2. **Family & Friendships**
   a. Y/N – 1st Priority
   b. Y/N – 2nd Priority

3. **Vocation**
   a. Y/N – 1st Priority
   b. Y/N – 2nd Priority

4. **Financial**
   a. Y/N – 1st Priority
   b. Y/N – 2nd Priority

TCRE 4Ts Final Key Decision

1. **Not Aligned w/ FG's multiple No's *No-Go**

   a. Why stmt. If No-Go Professionally/ Respectfully decline offer

2. **Aligned w/ FG's Yes *Go -Terms All Memorialized in Agreement **No Verbal**

   a. **Talent** – Clearly defined role w/ responsibility / accountability
      i. Details
   b. **Tools** – Necessary to perform role, Company Supplied/ Paid
      i. Details
   c. **Time** – Duration / Daily Commitment / Advancement / Exit strategy
      i. Details
   d. **Treasure** – Total Compensation
      i. Base Salary -
      ii. Performance Bonus -
      iii. Expenses Reimbursed w/ agreed cadence –
      iv. PTO –
      v. Benefits –
      vi. Other Measurable Comp -

Rules of the Road

Our Best Practice Values Shortlist:

Foundational Values	Service Professional Values
Authentic	Actively Engaged (Listen)
Balanced	Business Owner Oriented
Ethical	Committed to Overall Success
Fair	Excellence with Attention to Detail
Honest	Faithful and Realistically Optimistic
Integrity	Generous and Give More than you Receive
Loyal	Open Minded and Willing to Compromise
Optimistic	Organized and Prepared
Respectful	Results Focused
Trustworthy	Transparent with no Hidden Agendas

Our Professional Conduct Shortlist:

TalentCRE Methodologies	Continuing Education & Training
TCRE 4Ts Applications	Bachelors & Graduate Degree
TCRE Toolbox	Arch/ PE/ Real Estate/ MBA
TCRE PRISM Delivery	Public Speaking/ Presenting
TCRE 4Ts SWOT(T)	CAD/ Excel/ PPT/ Power BI
DART Program	Portfolio/ Workplace Strategy
Mentorship	Reading/ Online Content
Licenses & Certifications	**Memberships & Networking**
Architect (NCARB)	Non-Profit & Prof. Affiliations
Professional Engineer (PE)	Chamber of Commerce
Real Estate – Sales/ Broker	CoreNet/ NAR/ NAIOP
General Contractor GC/CM	BOMA/IFMA/NAHB/CCIM
PMP/CMCI/NCIDQ/CPM	Industry Events & Workshops
OSHA/ Green/ LEED/ Agile	Pick up the Phone * Say Hello

Appearance:

Remember best practice is to dress for your clients/ audience. Dress codes are based on working conditions and the effect your appearance will have on business relationships with other employees, people from other companies and the public. Standard dress should always be "business appropriate". This means different attire may be required based on your location, role and responsibilities. It is very important to let everyone know outwardly that you care about yourself and you have the confidence to show your unique self that projects Your Brand, Inc.

Scheduling:

Set a definite start and stop time for working, that means when you are done working for the day you unplug, you do not check emails or respond, you do not make or answer phone calls. You do not perform any work outside of agreed upon working hours, unless of course it is an emergency (rarely the case), or you want to write down an idea or something you just do not want to forget before the next day. Make this key decision today and you will be amazed how much time you free up for all your other FG's activities.

Our (WFH) - Remote & Office Environment List:

WFH - Remote	Office Environment
Set a defined start and stop time for working hours that everyone knows	Set a defined start and stop time for working hours that everyone knows
Create a distraction free and quiet work area	Starts before you enter the building, be respectful, friendly and polite
Work surface and surrounding area should be clean and clutter free	Know and abide by all safe workplace protocols
Make sure you have full access to computer, phone and network applications	Get to know your office site including security and facilities staff - make a quick ref. contact list
Have a solid background ideally away from traffic areas	Work surface and surrounding area should be clean and clutter free
Be aware of background noise and utilize headset to control	Participate in team events and always clean up after yourself
WFH is not a replacement for dependent care, if required make sure they do not significantly detract from your ability to perform your duties during working hours	Emergency readiness, know your Security and Safety Captains, have a complete understanding and be ready to go on all emergency procedures and evacuation routes
Pay attention to personal appearance and be fully dressed, with the ability to participate in a video meeting	Show up on time (that means 5 mins before official start) in proper attire for days activity with the ability to participate in any meeting
When you have an illness and cannot adequately perform your duties take PTO, no work including answering calls or responding to emails	When you are under the weather or have an illness where you can adequately perform your duties WFH is the best option, be considerate of your office mates
Make sure you hydrate, take breaks and get up from your seat to stretch your legs in the fresh air	Make sure you hydrate, take breaks and get up from your seat to stretch your legs in the fresh air

Our Meetings Best Practice List:

Meetings - Best Practices
Have a clearly defined agenda on meeting invite.
When invited to a meeting with no agenda, tentatively accept meeting requesting agenda, if not supplied respectfully decline meeting.
Durations should be ½-1 hour with tight agendas and have takeaway action items.
Maximum meetings per day no more than 4hrs in an 8–10-hour business day.
Total meeting attendance a week no more than 12-15hrs in a 45–50-hour work week unless you are participating in work sessions or special events.
Utilize reporting governance and meeting schedule cadence to avoid unnecessary meetings, if no required action items, send detailed status updates only.
Recurring Client meetings set for Tues-Thurs between 10am and 4pm during a standard Mon-Fri work week.
Establish a midpoint to your day with no recurring meetings, a 1hr break is required to maintain energy and focus (12-1pm works for most).
As the Subject Matter Expert (SME), you have the expertise. Manage from a place of authority, dictate the tone and value your expertise as a strategic and tactical partner.
Attendee list: Only invite key participants, no client sub-contractor team combined meetings, you are the Owner and must establish and maintain authority to provide clear direction on what is necessary to achieve objectives.
Try to avoid one-off client Key D (Decision) meetings, having a supporting team member present ensures dual control and the availability of witness if required.
Follow up Key D with Email (EM) confirmation, memorialize in Client/ Project mailbox, this establishes permanent record with no revisionary history.
Know your audience – Client/ Customer/ Contractor/ Vendor and adjust accordingly, you want to make sure content and delivery is well received.
Leverage Technology Platform - Audio/ Visual tools (MSFT 365, Google Workspace, Salesforce Customer 360, Oracle NetSuite, Zoom, etc..).
At beginning of multi-participant meetings keep conversation light/ appropriate especially when waiting for other participants and do not speak about other clients.
When presenting material or sharing your screen make sure all confidential or other non-relevant content is closed and not visible to the group.
Meeting notes should be sent/ published within 24hrs.
Celebrate Key Accomplishments & Victories no matter how small.
Keep Perspective, Be the Authentic You & Always end on Positive.

Our Technology Best Practice List:

Technology - Best Practices
Keep all equipment/ accessories in one designated place including all chargers and when required to be mobile have an organized carrying case that fits everything.
Utilize webcam cover to avoid not being visible when not participating in video call.
Always use secure Wi-Fi and make use of Virtual Private Network (VPN).
Create Strong Passwords with at least 8-10 characters example: !UP3lower9
Lock computer and mobile phone whenever you are not in front of or leave your work area, including WFH.
Set up voicemail on Mobile Phone with short personal message and adjust message when out on PTO, so people know you are out and when to expect a return call.
Set up/ Load Email on Mobile Phone ** Check at least 2x daily during work hours.
Have a 'System' for organizing/ prioritizing email, set up rules to increase efficiency and utilize delay delivery to align with agreed upon business hours.
Email Signature Line should have at minimum: Closing Salutation, Name, tel. #, EM.
Color code calendar with key categories for quick reference identification and delineation from different types of scheduled activities.
Schedule recurring task work meeting times and unplug when performing task work.
Email subject lines should be concise and content should only cover one related topic, not multiple unrelated. Start new threads and avoid continuous run-on emails.
When writing an email try to capture all or at least the most important content in the paragraph viewable size of standard email view, best chance of getting attention.
In Business communications – no emoji's/text short-hand (⊠, lol, ur, 2/to).
Email- Avoid replying all, reply only to Key participants (KP) until solution/ resolution is achieved. Especially with Clients unless KP, be considerate of everyone's inbox.
Email response time 24hr maximum, even if you do not have an answer yet, let them know you are working on it with a clear expectation of when you will complete.
When out on PTO identify backup resource & set up OOO message (email/ phone) with backup resource contact.
Naming convention for saving files: Date (YYMMDD) – Your Initials -Title -Subject, for example 210225-WK_TalentCRE_Client_ProjectMeetingMinutes.
If you modify/ update any file, update the file name with version number and your initials after the date. For example, if I noticed something wrong with Client Project Meeting Minutes and made an update, the format would follow: 210225v2-PS_TalentCRE_Client_ProjectMeetingMinutes.
No Phone Snubbing (Phubbing) when you are with clients, engaged in active conversation or participating in meetings. If you must look at phone, say excuse me, check quickly and close to lock screen.

Business Development:

- Getting to the Key Decision Maker

Training	New Pursuit – TCRE 4Ts Methodology

Pursuit Strategy – Get to Key Decision Maker (KDM)

Mindset - Think/ Act like a Business Owner and Leader

Goal – Get KDM Name

Perform - TCRE 4Ts SWOT(T)

- o **Talent**
  - Outline the organization from the CEO down, identify Department Leads in Finance, Operations, Sales/ Marketing (these people will be easier to access).
  - Outline their Competitors, Suppliers and Vendor Partners to understand their industry and who all the players are.
  - Determine the SWOT(T) for each department regarding its Sr. Leadership talent to assist in identify gaps you can fill, weaknesses to supplement or strengths to compliment.
- o **Tools**
  - Identify any proprietary tools they may be using or technology tools we already use.
  - Identify any unique/ distinct delivery services.
- o **Time**
  - In the research, know the businesses past and anticipate its needs for the future.
  - Stay updated on news/ trends to determine overall business strategy in relation to the environment, future product/ service offering demand and customer profiles.
  - Focus on innovations in product/ service delivery and impacts of season on cashflows, upcoming financial targets.
- o **Treasure**
  - Know their top clients.
  - Understand current CRE Portfolio and potential new sites.
  - New contracts underway or visibility into future work.
  - Strategic alliances you can access.

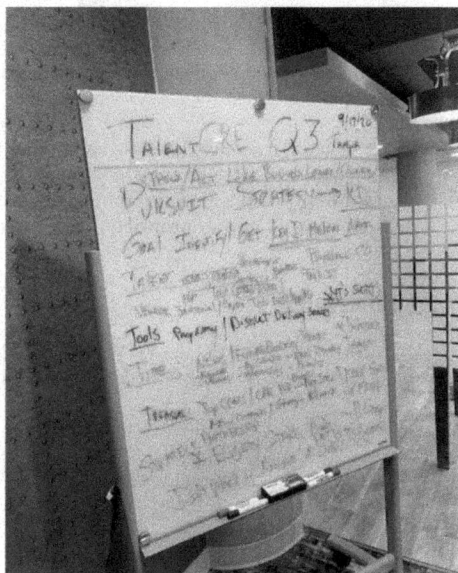

Training White Board Session

Key Takeaway: Perform full Due Diligence, approach the company as if you are going to take an Equity Stake or take over 100%; know the business; know the people; know their challenges and then when you get to the KDM, you can be positioned as a Strategic Partner peer providing a solution to their business needs and challenges with your unique service offering. Remember keep the 11 Step Success Plan front of mind and that we hire our clients.

TalentCRE

Business Development:

- Educational Sales Approach

Snapshot Example	Client Pursuit – Return to Office/ Change Mgmt.

Brief Summary

Completed due diligence on an IT firm New Client Pursuit Target and found out, in this time of COVID-19, that they have a myriad of long-term/ short-term leases in US East Coast major cities.

In the news, it seems like these companies may be losing money on unused spaces as their people work from home but still want to keep a footprint for in-person collaboration and work on confidential/ proprietary products and services.

Challenges

Talent - Attrition of talent if WFH flexibility is not allowed/ capable along with collaborative spaces.

Tools - Some technology can only be done on-site.

Time - Speed to market is critical at the IT firm, leases are short-term and long-term.

Treasure - Current space utilization is low; losing money with leased spaces (rent, utilities, Support Personnel), Brand may be compromised if unable to attract/ retain the best talent.

Results & Lessons Learned

Treasure - Renegotiate lease terms, include in marketing materials and HR, WFH flexibility policies and support including day care at office.

<u>Day In the Life</u>

Organization RTO/ Employee Change Mgmt.

TCRE 4Ts SWOT(T) – Assessment/ Options/ Best Path Forward.

Start - Review of Leases and space configuration, notify workforce that leadership is aware of the challenges and a program is underway to address these challenges.

Design - Engage SME to design space configuration to accommodate requirements and brokers to determine impacts. Engage workforce in design with surveys/ meetings to bring in their ideas and spur employee support and participation.

Build - Implement space designs and lease negotiations/ send regular updates to workforce of new changes and how to engage with updated spaces and technology.

Finish - Complete space configuration; Close negotiations; Reoccupy. Provide training to workforce on new upgrades/ changes; make available SME for training/ information.

Survey & Iteration - Gain feedback from workforce through surveys, focus groups and individual talks. Provide celebrations and recognition of hard work and highlight successes with future programs to come.

Result – Successful Safe Return to Office

TalentCRE

NEW CLIENT / BUSINESS PROTOCOL

Pre – Meet Answers

❑ **What Product / Service do we have that Client Needs?**

Answer:

❑ **Why do they need our Product / Service?**

Answer:

❑ **Why do they need our Product / Service Today (yesterday)?**

Answer:

Closing the Sale/ Contract

Mistake #1 - Never asking for the sale!

Mistake #2 - Not Listening!

TalentCRE

Sales Presentation – 11 Step Success Plan

- ☐ **Warm Up:** Familiarity *Anything but Business.
- ☐ **Determine Client Needs:** Questions & Answers *Listen
- ☐ **TalentCRE Story:** Why they called you & Personal reason why you are with TalentCRE.
- ☐ **Define Meeting Objective:** Introduce TCRE, Products / Services offered **Make it clear they will get a firm price & you are going to do business today.
- ☐ **Detail TCRE Service Platform:** Personalize to Individual / Client.
- ☐ **Detail TCRE Products Offered:** Personalize to Individual / Client.
- ☐ **Product Delivery Platform:** Circle of Risk Diagram / Story *TalentCRE Network Team Identification & CRE Services.
- ☐ **Present Price to Client:** Only answer questions, not responses or statements.
- ☐ **Close Sale-Sign Contracts:** Once Signed **Stop Selling!
- ☐ **Cool Down:** Assurances & Niceties.
- ☐ **Leave:** Happy & Humble.

TalentCRE

Remember

"Every Loss or Perceived Failure is an Opportunity to Learn How to Win and Succeed."

Goal – Closed Project Mgmt. Contract

Pre – Meet Answers:

o **What Product/ Service do we have that Client Needs?**
- After doing due diligence, the client needs project management services to lead the planning, design and new construction of a building.

o **Why do they need our Product/ Service?**
- They need our PM services – which is founded on the experience of our people, our results focused-ownership mentality, and our methodologies and tools – because their personnel are young and there is no one set of SOPs. The company needed our Project Management Services and Tools.

o **Why do they need our Product/ Service Today (Yesterday)?**
- This project is regulatory driven and a requirement by local government per tax incentives and needing completion in 24 months. The timing is now.

11 Step Success Plan (RFP Response & Presentation):

o **Warm Up**
- In the age of Zoom, Remote interviews may be more the case than not. During the setting up as people join, light conversation about a painting in the background of an interview warmed everyone up.

o **Determine Client Needs**
- As we opened our presentation, discussing the agenda and a brief introduction of the team and our services, we went directly into a Q/A sessions to determine what exactly was going on, the challenges the client was experiencing and how they saw the project play out. We listened, wrote down the challenges with the knowledge that we would address those specific challenges within the presentation – adding immediate value to their organizations and qualifying our abilities.

o **TalentCRE Story**
- After the Q/A session, we pause and say, "We'll talk about those challenges shortly, but just want to go into a little about ourselves, the team and why I'm part of it." After being at multiple staff augmentation CRE organizations, I decided to join TCRE where advisory/ strategic partnership were the focus. This allows me to act on the best interest of the client and provide CRE Excellence.

11 Step Success Plan (cont.):

- **Define Meeting Objective**
  - In this part, we discuss the overall services, products offered, our goal to win business and that at the end of the presentation, we'll discuss the rates, etc.

- **Detail TCRE Service Platform**
  - Following the above and based on the Q/A session, discussed our local expertise in the permitting process, our local footprint and network of vendors as well as our internal network of SMEs to ensure quality assurance of design and construction.

- **Detail TCRE Products Offered/ Delivery Platform (combined due to flow)**
  - As the presentation/ conversation continued and we describe how we can address permitting and knowledge of local vendors, we also sprinkle in our personal experiences with other organization – making sure to highlight the challenges of using local market resources with limited expertise and the impacts on budget, schedule and long-term relationships for future work.
  - This back and forth creates an idea in the client that without us and our experience, they may experience the same thing. We can help them not have that happen.

- **Present Price to Client**
  - As we close the presentation, wrapping up the challenges, our services and the risk of not having us, we presented our rates – highlighting any preferred client discounts provided and the transparency of our profits and our charitable contributions.
  - At this point, silence, we waited for questions – a few popped up but none that couldn't be answered. The key here was being transparent on the pricing and breaking down line items. There were a few comments, but we remained quiet – only answering questions, not adding to comments.

- **Close Sale – Sign Contracts**
  - A few days had passed where the client came back with clarifying questions but eventually awarded the contract to our team – signing and letting us begin.

- **Cool Downs/ Leave (combined due to virtual)**
  - Upcoming weekend talk and thank you notes were sent immediately after the presentation and after the award.

TalentCRE

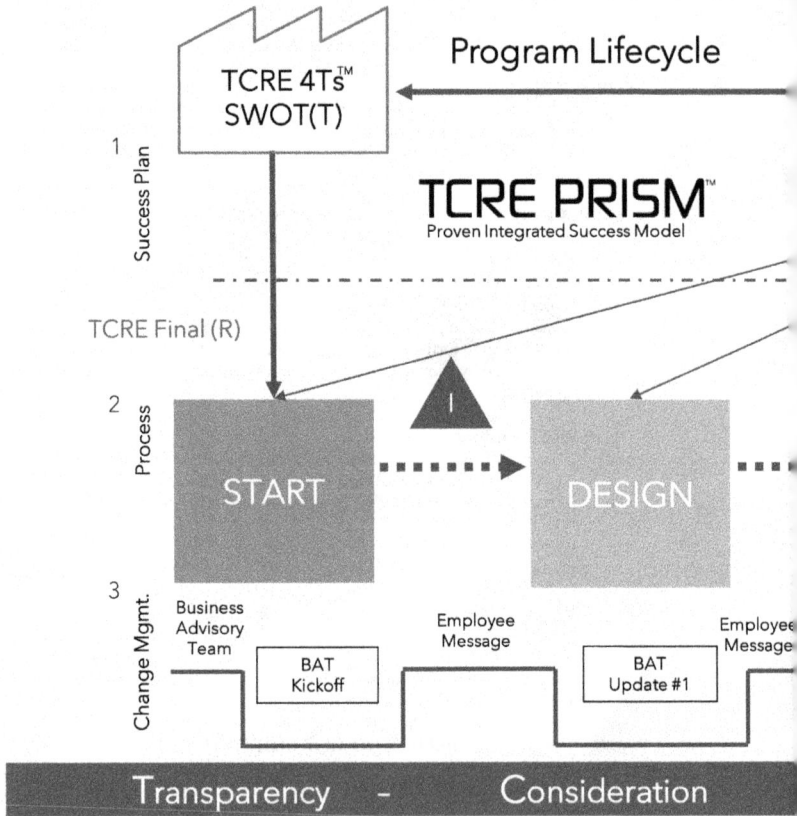

TalentCRE
An MWBE Commercial Real Estate Firm

TCRE 4Ts™ SWOT(T)

Program Lifecycle

TCRE PRISM™
Proven Integrated Success Model

1 — Success Plan

TCRE Final (R)

2 — Process

START

I

DESIGN

3 — Change Mgmt.

Business Advisory Team

BAT Kickoff

Employee Message

BAT Update #1

Employee Message

Transparency - Consideration

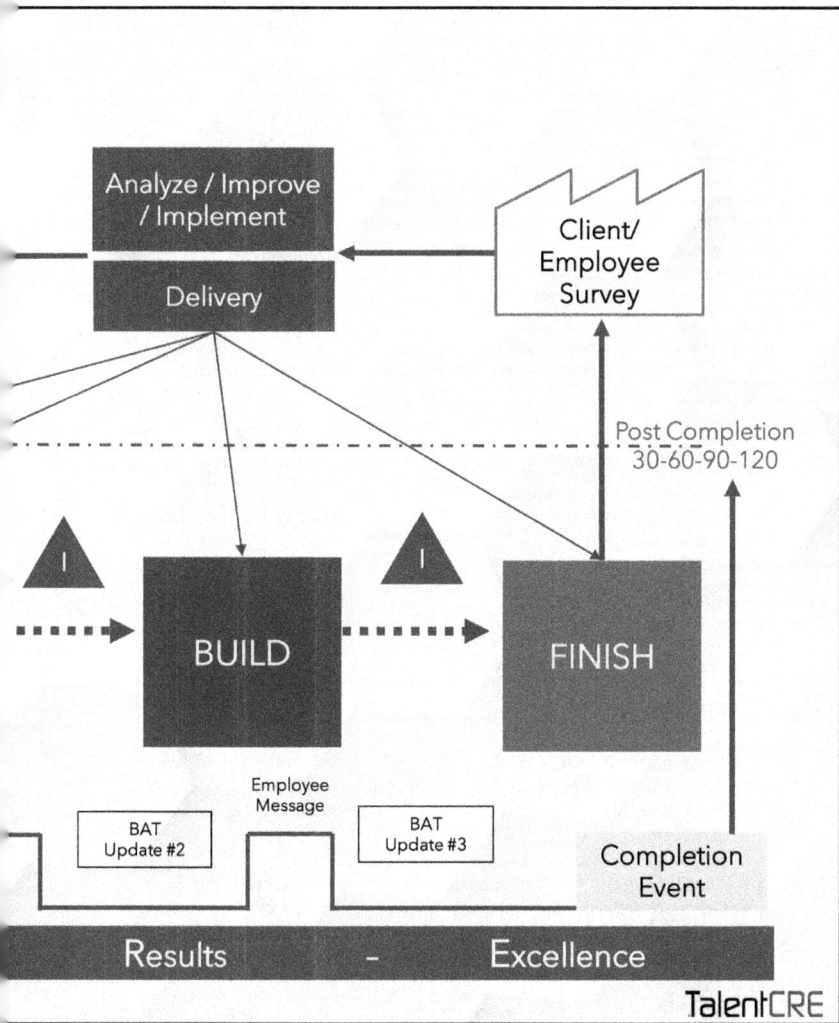

Analyze / Improve / Implement

Delivery

Client/ Employee Survey

Post Completion
30-60-90-120

I

I

BUILD

FINISH

Employee Message

BAT Update #2

BAT Update #3

Completion Event

Results — Excellence

TalentCRE

Application Example	TCRE Prism – Personal Success Plan

Goal – Implementation Framework for an Extraordinary Life

Success Plan:

- **TCRE 4Ts** = FG's Develop & Create Self Awareness/ Self Reflection/ Self Analysis
  - The process begins with an assessment of the current situation. In this case, its your life within the framework of the four foundational goals. How is your life going with regards to the four foundational goals? What is going well? What isn't?

- **TCRE Final (R)** = Locked FG's Memorialized
  - After the assessment, you should have a clear understanding of your strengths, weakness, opportunities, threats and trends in your life according to your foundational goals. Decide, according to your goals, where do you want to focus? What can be strengthened? What can you exploit now and leverage in your favor? What trends are happening and what should you do about them?
  - Lock your FG's – What are they? What needs help and how will you get there?
  - Example:
    - ❑ Health: Lose 25 lbs.
    - ❑ Family & Friends: Spend more time with Parents.
    - ❑ Vocation: Start new business.
    - ❑ Financial: Earn $75K this year.

Change Management:

- **Business Advisory Team** = Mentors/ Successful People you are Modeling.
  - While working your way through the goals – utilizing the Mentors and Successful people you're modeling – to give you feedback, guidance and inspiration.

- **Employee Message** = Releasing into the universe *Tell you Story.
  - Celebrate your victories with yourself and others. Let others know what is going well, but also let them know where you are struggling, what you are trying to do to over those struggles and how they can help.

Process:

- **Start** = Health FG's
  - As discussed in previous chapters, start with your Health FGs – because without breath or mental capacity, you can't do the other goals. Begin working your way through the goals – utilizing the Mentors and Successful people you're modeling – to give you feedback, guidance and inspiration.
  - Lose 25 lbs.
    - ❑ Set up exercise routine.
    - ❑ Join running group of successful runners.
- **Design** = Family & Friends FG's
  - Spend more time with Parents.
    - ❑ Set up lunch every Sunday.
    - ❑ Ask friends who have great relationships with parents what they do to stay connected.
- **Build** = Vocation FG's
  - Start a new Business.
    - ❑ Review personal finances and discuss risks with family.
    - ❑ Network with those who not only started a similar business but any business for experiences and lessons learned.
- **Finish** = Financial FG's
  - Earn $75K per year.
    - ❑ Increase skills in industry and salary negotiation.
    - ❑ Network with those in your industry a level or two above you to find out what they did.

Success Plan Review/ Update:

- **Employee Survey** = Self-Analysis / Measuring Results
  - Check in and be real with yourself. How are you doing? What's going well? What isn't? What are you going to do about it?
- **Analyze/ Improve/ Implement** = Refine/ Commit/ Continue/ Believe & Achieve
  - After the check-in, which can be the 4Ts Assessment again, revise your Process and implement whatever needs to be addressed.

TalentCRE

| Application Example | TCRE Prism – Business Advisory/ Program Mgmt. |

Brief Summary: In Q2 of 2020, XYZ Business requested an assessment and implementation plan to return to work during the COVID 19 crisis. The company specializes in information technology (IT) services and are supported by day to day operational/ admin services.

Goal – Safe Return to Work while maintaining business continuity/ profitability.

Success Plan:

o **TCRE 4Ts** = Business Assessment
  - A complete assessment of the business was conducted determined that they were strong in Talent, Tools and Treasure but weak with Time – as the company had planned to return to their office by Q4 2020 but being it was Q2, planning was already behind.

o **TCRE Final (R)** = 3 Options with a Final Recommend
  - Utilizing the assessment as a foundation, three options were created on how the company should position their real estate and return to work. Our company provided a recommendation for final approval by the client.

Change Management:

o **Business Advisory Team**
  - Continuous communication with Executive Sponsor and Lines of Business Leads.

o **Employee Message**
  - Distribution of newsletters, townhalls and furniture mockups for employee change management.

o **Post Completion**
  - Days during the lifecycle for events to occur.

Process (snapshot detail):

- **Start**
  - Kickoff & Goal Alignment.
  - Due Diligence/ Site-Visits.
  - Complete Speed Charter.
  - Lease Abstract.

- **Design**
  - Scope Definition.
  - Review / Approve SD's / DD's / CD's.
  - RFP's Vendors/ Award Contracts.
  - Lock Build (Scope/ Budget/ Schedule).

- **Build**
  - Assoc. Moves/ FFE Removal.
  - Demo/ Construction.
  - FFE Install.
  - Testing/ Commissioning.

- **Finish**
  - Punchlist Complete.
  - FM Handoff.
  - Occupy Move In.
  - Final Invoices/ Unconditional Lien Waiver.
  - Final Close Package.

Success Plan Review/ Update:

- **Employee Survey**
  - Asking the workforce how they are doing? How were the moves and/ or new equipment? Get feedback to address and plan for future projects.

- **Analyze/ Improve/ Implement**
  - With the feedback from the Executive Sponsor, Internal project teams and Workforce, refine the analysis, implementation and change management processes for future programs.

TalentCRE

TCRE 4Cs

Communication – If we are not talking (all forms) there is absolutely no way for us to know or understand what is required of us to collectively succeed. When we start communicating effectively and have deep dialogue around all aspects of the ins outs of what is happening (forces internal and external), we can then start solutioning by means of the next C.

Collaboration - Everyone needs to work together in a positive respectful manner, leveraging their expertise and unique experience. Collectively we are better at problem solving and can be more effective, efficient and achieve at a far higher level than if we are working in silos or apart with competing agendas.

Consistency - Show up, day in and day out, as a known trusted commodity able to be counted on, committed to the team, process and the end goal.

Closeout – Finish everything you are responsible for. Every task you start, you track the progress and see it through to the end, ensuring that everything is completely done and nothing falls through the cracks.

simplification - Continuously identify ways to make things easier and less complicated. Focus on increased efficiencies that will lead to faster delivery and enhanced results.

Competitive!

To be successful you must be competitive and have a competitive spirit where you are 100% committed to Winning no matter what the obstacles or perceived competitor stands in your way. Notice we said perceived competitor not competitor or competition. This is because we believe whole heartedly that:

"The only Competition you have in Life, is to be the Best You."

10

Inspired & Energized

We are so grateful that the people in our lives and our unique life experiences have led us to the point, where we have acquired enough courage, valuable knowledge and confidence to bring together some of the ideas, life lessons and proven actionable strategies that have allowed us to prosper and to live an Extraordinary Victorious Life.

Our hope is that you have enjoyed the book, learned more about yourself, identified the unique gifts you possess and have gained a deeper understanding of the people, situations and experiences that have impacted your life and the role your conscious choices have on your life and others.

You have also learned how you can model what others have utilized to achieve great results and tailor them specifically to align with your foundational goals, knowing with absolute certainty that you are now armed with the Talent, Tools, Time and Treasure for achieving an Extraordinary Victorious Life where you

Strive:

- **To be the Best You.**

- **To be 100% Present & Committed to Your Chosen Foundational Goals.**

- **For Quality over Quantity.**

- **To Remember There are No Bad Experiences in Life Just Unpleasant Ones.**

- To Practice the Law of Attraction and Positivity.

- To Do Unto Others as You Would Have Them Do Unto You.

- To Always Give More Than You Receive.

- For Balance/ Strength/ Endurance/ Flexibility in Every Aspect of Your Life.

Life is an Endurance Challenge, Not a Sprint. Celebrate the Victories and the Losses, knowing that with every passing Moment/ Step, every Relationship and Experience (ups/ downs), you are on a Purposeful Quest Living the Extraordinary Victorious Life you have Choose and were Destined to Lead.

"Enjoy Sharing Your Favorite Slice of Cake with The World."

Thank You

About Authors:

David Wick is a lifelong entrepreneur in spirit and practice who is deeply committed to helping people personally and professionally in every environment he finds himself.

He is responsible for global strategy and executive leadership of our Talent Network, Business Advisory and Project Management Services business at TalentCRE, Inc. David has held key leadership positions throughout his career as well as owned and operated multiple businesses within CRE, design build construction, tradesman services and business advisory. He has been involved in the development and delivery of more than $1B in real estate and has successfully turned around countless dark red programs/ projects.

David has been fortunate to experience all of life's wonderful gifts for the last 28 years with his wife and two sons who ensure every day is full of love, comedy and excitement. If you would like to connect with him, please send a note to wick@talentcre.com

Pablo Sierra is a Navy veteran, business owner and commercial real estate professional whose expertise in advisory services and project management aligns strategies with assets and implementation activities – resulting in stronger companies and long-term value.

He has worked with a variety of clients in the public and corporate sectors – including the US Department of Defense, US Department of Education, Bank of America, Capital One Financial and Exelon – developing and implementing project management offices (PMOs), leading real estate project teams and establishing project portfolio management models and governance processes.

Pablo is a graduate of the US Naval Academy in Annapolis, MD and a former Naval Officer. He is currently leading the Business Advisory Service Line at TalentCRE, helping clients overcome challenges and recognize their full business value by assessing, identifying and optimizing their portfolio of talent, tools and assets.

He is happily married, with a son and living his best life. He can be reached at sierra@talentcre.com

Index

www.ingramcontent.com/pod-product-compliance
Lightning Source LLC
Chambersburg PA
CBHW070756300326
41914CB00053B/693